I0453863

QUICKSAND - MURDER UNRESOLVED

Quicksand - Murder Unresolved

EDMOND N GAGNON

Copyright © 2025 by Edmond Gagnon
All rights reserved. No part of this book may be reproduced in any
manner whatsoever without written permission except in the case
of brief quotations embodied in critical articles and reviews.
First Printing, 2025
Although this book may have been inspired by an actual occur-
rence, all persons, places and events in this story are fictitious or
imagined by the author.
Cover Art by Author Edmond Gagnon
Edited by Christine Hayton

Other Books by Edmond Gagnon

A Casual Traveler

Four - A Paranormal Thriller

Norm Strom Crime Series

Rat
Bloody Friday
Torch
Finding Hope
Border City Chronicles
Trafficking Chen
Border City Chronicles - Four More
Melaque Murder Club

Abigail Brown Crime Series

Moon Mask
Millionaire Murders

For the physically and verbally abused...

Part I

Hit & Run

Chapter One

The Red Car

Weekday mornings were chaotic. Annie Gladstone Daniels loved children, especially her own, but getting them moving and ready for school made her wonder if she shouldn't have chosen a dog or cat instead. Their father was still in the picture, but even before the separation he wasn't much help when it came to dealing with the responsibility of child rearing.

Eight and nine years of age, Ashley and Christopher were quite capable of fending for themselves but chose to rely on mom whenever they could get away with it. Believing it was part of the job description, Annie usually caved to their demands. She often felt they were pushing the envelope just to see exactly how far she would go. *Kids,* she thought, *they can be hard to live with but I could not live without them.*

It was as if they were teenagers already, or so it seemed. Christopher talked back like he knew it all, and Ashley told her mother she didn't know what it was like to be the only girl in the family. Annie reminded her daughter they were the same gender, and she'd grown up with more than one

1

brother. She secretly wished the children would never get older but on the other hand, couldn't wait for them to become more self-sufficient.

As if she didn't have enough to worry there was Dale, her estranged husband; the last-minute cancellations when he was supposed to pick up the kids, non-stop phone calls, messages, and emails. He snuck around the house when she was at work, leaving suggestive love notes and even following and stalking her. Annie had grown afraid of her one-time best friend and husband

Annie and Dale had chosen to live in Cooperville for its proximity to the children's grade school. When he was in the picture, it was her husband's job to drop them off in the morning on the way to his job at the chemical plant. Things changed after the separation and Annie adjusted her hours at work so she could drive the kids to and from school. Buses were available but that would have complicated their morning ritual even more.

The Daniels' climbed into the family minivan a few minutes behind schedule, as usual. Annie fumbled in her purse for the keys but remembered she left them in the house. It seemed she was always losing things in the giant bag or forgetting where she left stuff. Christopher went back into the house while mom checked herself in the mirror to make sure she hadn't forgotten to put makeup on. Annie wondered if her memory would get any worse with age.

The morning sun peeked over the horizon in a cloudless sky. Spring had sprung but the cool night left dew on the minivan's windows. That time of year in Cooperville was unpredictable. You could cross-country ski one day and take out your bicycle the next. It was the lake effect in the southern tip of Ontario, a peninsula surrounded by Lake St. Clair, the Detroit River, and Lake Erie.

Annie started the engine, switched on the wipers, and headed for the kids' school. Arriving at their drop-off point with other tardy parents was a good thing since the lineup was shorter than usual. Ashley kissed her mother goodbye, but Christopher was already out the door. At the beginning of the last school year, he told his mother he was too old for that mushy stuff.

Annie checked her watch as she pulled from the curb, and headed to her Assistant Librarian position at the town library. An avid reader, she had always loved hanging out in book stores or libraries. Whether growing up at home, or living alone in her first apartment, Annie always had a shelf full of books she'd either read, or planned on reading.

She coaxed the van above the speed limit to make up for lost time. Annie was hosting a class of students from an area school who were coming to see the newly renovated Cooperville Library. After asking her boss if she could take on more responsibility in order to learn everything there was to know about the job, Annie gained the title of Library Tour Guide.

The loud roar didn't register, her mind was elsewhere. *Did Christopher lock the door before they left? Would Dale sneak in and snoop around the house again? She had to call the doctor and change her appointment. Not sure what there was in the freezer.* Annie wondered what she'd make for dinner. She saw the school kids neatly lined up in front of the library, waiting for her.

The paved road out front of the library was free of traffic. Annie was running a bit behind schedule and the children's school bus had moved on. If it wasn't for the chattering of the kids in line, the neighborhood outside the library would have been as quiet outside as it was inside.

Parked on the shoulder of the road, Annie got out of her minivan and walked toward the library. She took in a deep breath of country air but hesitated for a moment, thinking her phone was vibrating. About to check her purse, Annie remembered putting it in her pocket. Standing in the middle of the road, she heard a loud noise. It was a red car bearing down on her. Annie noticed the birds stopped chirping and she could no longer hear the children for the noise of the car engine. The air seemed perfectly still. Her peripheral vision took in the azure blue of the sky above and the forest green of grass and shrubbery around her. Her focus was on the approaching vehicle. It hadn't been there a few seconds earlier, when she got out of her van. But there it was. A huge black grill, like the gaping mouth of a killer whale. Annie had been walking toward the library but apparently not quickly enough. It didn't make any sense. *Did the driver not see me?* She saw him. Their gaze locked for a second. The imminent danger she was in didn't seem to register with him.

Annie Gladstone Daniels always put everyone else first. She thought about the school children near the roadway, wondering if they were safe. A feeling of helplessness washed over her. *What about Ashley and Christopher, who would take care of them if something happens to me? Surely not Dale. He never really wanted kids and it didn't take long for him to show it.* Flashbacks of her childhood raced through Annie's mind; good memories.

Why isn't the car stopping? Why don't my legs move faster so I can get out of the way? Annie tried to move quicker but it was as if the pavement melted and her feet sunk into it. Her legs and the rest of her body wasn't responding either, like she'd lost control of her reflexes. *What's happening to me...is this for real or am I still at home in bed, dreaming?*

For a split second in time, Annie wished she could simply slip below the surface of the earth to a better place. Then there was pain. All-encompassing pain, as if she was shrink-wrapped in heavy plastic and it was squeezing the life out of her. Like a freed balloon lost to the clouds, Annie drifted above the library in a state of semi-consciousness.

She saw nothing but darkness; outer space without the Milky Way. There were feelings of dread. Emptiness. A flash of hope came in the form of unrecognizable voices that faded in and out. But none of the words made any sense. *Is someone here with me?* She felt alone. It was as if her body was present but her mind packed up and left town.

Annie searched and wandered about in the emptiness but couldn't find her way out of it. Images of her children, parents, and siblings popped up out of nowhere and appeared as photographs on an endless black wall. They offered her warmth, a feeling she was loved. *Is it a sign of hope that I would see them all again? Where are they? Where am I?*

A faint white light appeared in the distance. Annie Daniels struggled with all her might to move closer to it. Paralyzed, she couldn't move.

Am I really melting into the roadway to avoid that car? This is a bad dream. It explains the suffocating pain and darkness enveloping me. It was as if she'd been swallowed by quicksand.

Chapter Two

Little Samantha

Samantha Evans was a bookworm, super-excited to visit the new library. Her mother had left her at the old library several times in the past while she went shopping nearby. The young girl liked to swap books she'd already read and flipped through women's fashion magazines when her mom wasn't around.

A shy girl at heart, Samantha lived through many of the books she read. At nine years old, the child felt she was much too mature for the children's stories her mother steered her to read. Samantha normally checked out age-appropriate books to satisfy her mom but always tucked a copy or two of National Geographic in between.

Samantha stood near the shoulder of the road, helpless and fearing the inevitable. Mrs. Daniels was about to be hit by a car. At her age, she didn't know much about cars or how fast they were supposed to go. She winced at what she saw was about to happen. The speeding car was red, similar to the nail polish her mother wore, and it resembled the race cars her dad watched on television.

A little taller, but less outgoing than her schoolmates, she was one of the visiting children who'd just been dropped off at the town library and was waiting for a tour of the new building. Samantha and Ashley Daniels were on the same soccer team. She recognized her friend's mother getting out of the minivan across the street. Excited to greet her or maybe warn her, Samantha broke ranks and started toward the road.

The young girl saw the red car and its driver, a man, but his face was blurred. She wondered why he didn't slow down or see Mrs. Daniels, who was in the middle of the road. Samantha tried calling out to her friend's mother but it was too late. The car slammed into her and she flew into the air. Samantha thought it was weird how the car moved so fast but it appeared Mrs. Daniels moved in slow motion.

The driver must have known he hit someone but didn't bother to stop. Mrs. Daniels landed in a shallow ditch on the side of the road. Samantha ran to her to see if she could help. Ashley's mom laid motionless in the ditch, her head resting on a cement curb. Samantha saw how badly she was hurt, bleeding and moaning.

Samantha felt angry and sorry at the same time. It was like when her brother ran over her doll with his bicycle, but worse because Mrs. Daniels was a real person. She thought about Ashley. Would someone tell her what happened to her mother?

A teacher grabbed her by the arm and led her back to the library. She said help was on the way but Samantha wanted to do more. What if it was her mother lying there? All the children were ushered into the building. A short time later she heard sirens and hoped it was an ambulance to take Mrs. Daniels to the hospital.

Other children in her class saw the accident too. Some of them cried. One girl was so upset she got sick and fainted. Their teacher and the head librarian tried to keep the kids corralled but some of them pressed their noses against the big windows, trying to see what was happening outside. Flashing lights lit up their young curious faces.

The children were told they'd be sent back to school as soon as their bus arrived to pick them up. A police officer entered the library and spoke to Samantha's teacher. Miss Thatcher pointed at her and two other children. He took the three of them to a separate room and asked what they had seen outside the library.

Samantha and Tommy blurted out their versions of the event but Lori remained quiet and began to cry. Overwhelmed by different versions of the same event, the police officer talked to someone on his radio and asked the children to remain there while he tried to contact their parents. Samantha heard another siren and hoped Mrs. Daniels would be okay.

Chapter Three

911

Chaos, confusion, and crying best describe the scene around the new library. It was a whole lot of action for the small and normally quiet town of Cooperville. A second ambulance joined the posse of police cars and fire trucks. Besides taking care of Annie Daniels, paramedics tended to and checked on the well-being of the children.

Someone had pushed the panic button, lighting up phone lines at the area's 911 Call Center. There were several similar calls reporting a hit and run, woman hit and thrown into the air, pedestrian struck, hysterical children, and a stolen car. With all the distressed people gathered and emergency vehicles, the usually quiet neighborhood quickly became a disaster scene.

Normally a place where only hushed voices and whispers were allowed, the library morphed into a triage center for distraught children and worried parents who'd been summoned to the scene. Police investigators received conflicting descriptions of the vehicle's driver who ran down Annie Daniels. The general consensus was it was no accident.

It wasn't that the children gave poor descriptions of the car or person driving it, just very different ones. From all accounts, the driver was indeed a male. The vehicle was reported to be a muscle car, possibly an older model Camaro or Firebird, red, like the one Tommy Lions said his brother had.

One of the adult witnesses said the suspect vehicle had been idling in a vacant parking lot down the street prior to the incident. According to her, the driver revved the engine before he drove directly at Annie Daniels. Acting on that information, police conducted a search of the area to locate the red car. It was found a short time later, abandoned only a few blocks away.

Another witness saw the man who walked away from the 1970 SS Camaro. He was described as being average in height and weight, casually dressed, with fair hair. It wasn't his vehicle. The car's owner had reported its theft from a nearby convenience store. Apparently, it was his daily routine to leave the engine running while he bought cigarettes and checked his lottery tickets.

Police noted fresh damage to the hood and grill, believed to have been caused when the car struck Annie Daniels. They impounded the Camaro for forensic testing, hoping to find further evidence of the collision and possibly who was driving it. The convenience store clerk confirmed the owner of the car was buying smokes, and his vehicle was out front when someone drove off with it.

Chapter Four

Cooperville

I met my best friend for breakfast at Elias Deli in downtown Windsor. Jesse and I had known each other since high school, but worked in separate areas most of our careers with the police service. We rarely got to share a meal together. We were near the same age and size but he was always in better shape than me, spending more time at the gym.

Jesse had a court appearance and popped by my office to talk me into breakfast. It wasn't hard. He knew it was my favorite meal of the day. I'd been typing reports on an arson case I was investigating and welcomed the break. He'd left the investigative jobs behind and opted for a more leisurely role as one of the sergeants in the cell control area.

Other cops frequented the restaurant throughout the day for coffee or meal breaks so it wasn't unusual for one of them to stop by our table. Karl Dean had a lot less time on the job than Jesse and I. The Windsor Police Service wasn't that big and many of us knew each other. There were always new hires whom we didn't have any contact with.

Dean and I both owned Harley Davidson motorcycles and had been on some group rides together. Assigned to the Traffic Division as an Accident Reconstructionist, he stopped by to say hello on his way out of the restaurant. "Hey, Norm, I'm headed out to your old neck of the woods...a nasty hit and run near the library in Cooperville. The locals have asked for help."

"You bringing your geometry set and crayons?"

Jesse was busy filling his face but chuckled with his mouth full and nodded to Dean.

It took him a second but Dean came back. "Does your boss know you played with matches and started fires when you were a kid?"

Jesse rolled his eyes from Dean to me. It was a story that very few people knew about and I wasn't quite sure if the traffic cop was messing with me or he actually knew something of my past. I smirked and waved him off. My best friend finished his glass of milk and leaned in closer. "Is he talking about the time you set the field behind your house on fire?"

I used my fork to corral the last bit of corned beef hash on my plate. "I don't think so...he's gotta be pulling my chain. There's no way he could know...I don't think he was even born yet."

Jesse and I spent the first half of our careers in uniform and later years in investigative jobs. Neither one of us ever had any interest in traffic enforcement, where the job meant writing speeding tickets all day. Accident reconstruction was something certain officers specialized in, after taking specific training. They became technicians who took measurements and photographs at serious or fatal collision scenes so that the incident could be 'reconstructed' to prove fault or liability.

I never thought any more about Dean's call out to Cooperville or the hit and run. There was only one traffic signal in town so I assumed someone blew a red light. I lived there for about six years enjoying country living but had recently moved back to the city. It was a nice break living near the lake but after my marriage ended and my mother passed, I saw no reason to remain out there by myself.

The rest of my family, friends, and job were in the city. Being on call 24/7 in the Arson Unit made the drive back and forth at all hours a pain in the ass. After moving back to the city, the only things I regretted leaving behind were the pond and gardens I had built from scratch in my back yard.

The town itself was a small lakeside village, once a retreat for many Americans who crossed the border to build summer cottages. Many of them renovated or winterized, making them fulltime homes. Others were bulldozed to make room for something better. My place was only a half dozen houses from Lake Erie, on a quiet street that ended at a park on the waterfront.

A city boy for almost all of my life, I moved to Cooperville and bought my mother a house only four doors down when she decided to relocate from out west. She was close enough to keep an eye on but far enough away that I didn't have to see her every day. We shared a passion for gardening and I played the good son role by doing little chores or driving her for groceries.

Jesse got up to use the bathroom. "You miss living out there?"

I shrugged. "I missed you."

He laughed. "Yeah, you missed the corned beef hash more."

Chapter Five

The Gladstones

Everyone who knew Annie Gladstone described her as cheerful and optimistic. A petite woman with an infectious smile. Strawberry blonde hair and green eyes personified shyness but she routinely went out of her way to start a conversation and make those around her feel comfortable. Her physical attributes contrasted with those of her siblings, and they joked she was a product of the milkman.

Along with her brothers and sister, Annie worked in the family store from the time she was old enough to push a broom. The candy section was her favorite, where inventory never seemed to match up with sales. Her parents, Joe and Marie Gladstone, owned Corner Convenience & Gas.

It was a one-stop shop where you could gas up your car, have a flat tire repaired, grab a few groceries, baked or canned goods. There was a small lunch counter at the back of the store where you could have a bowl of soup or fresh-made sandwich. People camping in the area would stop by for ice or necessities and bags of firewood.

Jimmy and Joe Junior resembled younger versions of their father, JJ at bit taller and rounder than his younger brother.

They worked the gas pumps and did oil changes or fixed flat tires in the garage around back. Sarah worked the cash register and Annie helped at the lunch counter when she was old enough. Customers loved her and left generous tips, something her older sister complained about until she was cut in on the action.

Joe Senior was the grill man and he managed the entire operation. Besides keeping the books, Marie crafted homemade soups and sandwiches to keep regular lunch customers coming back for more. She also made her own baked goods. Everyone played their part in the family business, covering for each other when things like school got in the way.

When business was slow, Annie read books. As many as she could get her hands on. They had a shelf where customers could take or leave a book, giving her a never-ending supply of fresh reading material. She visited the library whenever she could and hoped to one day become a Librarian. It was all about the books. She loved their smell and admired the endless shelves and rows of neatly stacked titles from authors all over the world.

Joe and Marie's Corner Convenience & Gas Bar was a family business, a place where their children learned about life; important lessons about loyalty, respect, and responsibility. The Gladstones watched their offspring carry those lessons into adulthood, as they took on careers and started families of their own. Family was always important to Annie and she hoped to have her own children someday.

Chapter Six

No Accident

What I thought was a simple motor vehicle accident in Cooperville turned out to be a hit and run and left a young woman in the hospital, fighting for her life. I did a double-take when I recognized her name in the newspaper. Annie Gladstone Daniels. I didn't know her well, but had chatted with her on occasion when I popped into the family store in Cooperville for gas or a snack.

Our casual conversations were often flirtatious on my end but I was faithful to my wife. Annie always loaded up my chicken salad sandwich when I stopped in for a bag lunch on my way to the city for the afternoon shift. She was easy to look at and had obviously gotten married at some point since I'd last seen her.

I was completely shocked when I read that she'd been run down intentionally by a man in a stolen car. Disgusted and shaking my head, I wondered who could do something like that to such a sweet woman. As a cop, I wondered why. Having been witness to the darkness in people, seeing the shitty things they did to each other for my twenty-something years on the job, I really wasn't surprised.

It reminded me of the early days in my police career, when I worked in patrol and investigated motor vehicle collisions. I only investigated one fatality I could remember. Seeing dead people is not easy to forget. Two pickup trucks had collided at Riverside Drive and Walker Road, the smaller one was ripped in half and the woman driver was dead on our arrival. Expecting blood and gore, I was amazed there was barely a mark on her. Her neck was broken. I'd investigated several hit and run collisions where, most often, the driver wasn't caught until sometime later.

I remembered a call to the old Windsor Market on Chatham Street. The victim said he was trying to exit his car when another vehicle sideswiped his, tearing the driver's door right off. Able to catch the license plate, he passed it on to me. To follow up, I attended a residence in Remington Park and knocked on the door where the fleeing vehicle was registered. An elderly man wearing a patch over his right eye answered the door. He had no idea why a policeman was at his house, and said he knew nothing about hitting another car. His wife joined us on the way to the garage when I asked to see his vehicle.

The whole passenger side of their car was heavily damaged. When I asked the old woman if she was with her husband in the car near the city market, she only offered me a stunned expression. The gentleman admitted she was with him, and apologized for her not answering my question because she was completely deaf. It only took me a second to realize she didn't hear the collision, and with his limited vision, he obviously didn't see the other car.

I figured the Cooperville cops would have their hands full, being such a small police service. I wondered if they would reach out beyond Karl Dean for investigative expertise. Windsor Police didn't typically help smaller towns in the area. They would reach out to the Queen's Regional Police or on rare occasion in federal matters, the Royal Canadian Mounted Police.

According to the paper, police had few leads and no suspects. Knowing that investigators normally held certain details from the general public, I wondered what they really knew and how quickly they'd have the asshole in bracelets. The article said Annie Gladstone was struck in broad daylight and it appeared to be intentional. Several children witnessed the hit and run and gave descriptions of the driver.

I had investigated my share of motor vehicle collisions over the years, including hit and runs, but I couldn't recall ever investigating one that was done intentionally. That was attempted murder, no doubt about it. A criminal investigation like that would go beyond Dean's expertise and I wondered if the Cooperville Police could handle it on their own.

I scanned the newspaper article again to see if I missed anything. No other names were listed as possible suspects. The rumor at work was one of our guys had started dating Annie just before she was killed and he had been questioned by investigators. I knew the man, having worked with him in Street Crimes. How well do we really know anyone? Regardless, I was confident he wasn't responsible for the hit and run.

Chapter Seven

Brotherly Love

Joe Junior was at work when he got a phone call from his father. He said there was a hit and run and Annie was taken to the hospital. It was as if someone punched him square in the diaphragm and he lost his breath. He imagined the worst, even though his dad didn't elaborate. JJ wondered if Annie didn't already have enough problems dealing with her estranged husband and custody issues.

His chest tightened and he could hear his own heartbeat. JJ didn't remember the drive to the hospital but can't forget the scary thoughts that raced through his mind. They were all about Dale; not just rumors but stories he'd heard and behavior he witnessed himself. He believed that his brother-in-law was cheating on his sister even before their actual separation.

The information fell into his lap at work one day. He worked for an auto parts supplier and delivered engine parts to the Ford Motor plant. It was the same company where Dale Daniels worked. According to JJ's source, his brother-in-law's affair was no secret at the factory. On several occasions, he was seen consorting with a female co-worker.

Loving his sister to death, JJ initiated his own investigation. He wanted all the facts before he approached Annie with bad news. He'd accepted Dale as part of the family when his sister first brought him around, but his blatant indiscretions enraged the eldest brother. He and Jimmy had always looked after Annie the best they could, like big brothers were supposed to.

Seeing the expression on his parents' faces, JJ took another gut punch. It was round two when he arrived at the hospital and he thought he was having a heart attack. He felt nauseous and had to sit down. Jimmy was there consoling his sister, Sarah, and his parents were sitting so close together it appeared they were sharing the same seat.

Someone addressed the family; he can't remember if it was a doctor or nurse. Annie's injuries were so severe, they said they were shipping her to the trauma unit at a Detroit hospital. Technically, Dale was still Annie's spouse so Sarah made phone calls, trying to reach him. He returned the call and according to her, seemed more concerned about where the accident happened instead of how his wife was.

Sarah said Dale's words sounded forced, like he was acting or on downers. The statement made JJ think about his brother-in-law's past behavior, when Dale was either drinking or smoking pot or on anti-depressants and crying in front of his children.

Jimmy Gladstone was enjoying his day off and working out downstairs in his personal gym. He didn't hear the telephone. Returning upstairs after the workout, Jimmy checked his messages and listened to one from his father. It said to call him back as soon as possible, Annie had been involved in an accident. He showered and drove to the Windsor hospital, still dripping wet.

From the moment he initially spoke to his father on the phone, he prayed to God in his head, *please, don't let her die.* Jimmy said the five days in the hospital were the worst days of his life. The waiting and hoping for good news, which never came.

The family was all there, along with two paramedics Jimmy knew. Two well-dressed strangers who turned out to be police detectives, were also there. His family filled him in on details of the hit and run. He never considered the possibility of Dale's involvement until the detectives mentioned they wanted to talk to him.

The Gladstone family piled into JJ's van to follow Annie to the Detroit hospital. The hit and run made the news, it was on the radio. They all gathered in the waiting room, joined by other extended family. Their initial contact with the doctor was not positive. There was no good news and they prepared for the worst.

Jimmy was shocked when they were finally allowed to see Annie. She had never regained consciousness and was hooked up to all sorts of wires and tubes and machines. Half of her head was shaved and the permanent smile Annie normally wore was now only a memory. It was heartbreaking to see his little sister in that surreal condition. Her broken appearance reminded him of her favorite doll after his father accidentally ran it over with his car.

Frozen in time, Jimmy could only stare at his sister and remember better days. Like the time she said she was old enough to work in the kitchen and he named her Toast Master. It was her job to butter toast for breakfast and she made the job look like an art project, carefully working the butter into all four corners of the bread. She once asked if she was supposed to cut the crust off.

Jimmy cracked a smile at the memory. The uplifted corners of his mouth caught tears that ran down his face. There were so many other sweet memories but he suddenly felt sick to his stomach and quickly turned to leave the room. Other family members were still gathered out in the waiting area.

The police detectives returned at some point and said they had spoken to Dale. They found him at his girlfriend's house. Most of that day was a blur but Jimmy recalled his mother on the phone with Dale. He grabbed it and his brother-in-law repeated the phrase, "What do I do, what do I do?" Jimmy hated him more than anything at that point. He screamed out, "Fucking asshole!"

Chapter Eight

Office Scuttlebutt

Sammy Fiorino plopped his ass into the chair occupying the temporarily vacant cubicle across from mine in the Financial Crimes Office. I was the single man Arson Unit, situated in the same office. Sammy was a detective with the Queen's Regional Police Property Crime Unit and we worked a couple of joint force operations together, dealing with B & E's in and around the county.

The first JFO was in the Town of Belle River, where Sammy and I worked with the QRP Mobile Surveillance Unit to track a known criminal who was doing break-ins in the town's residential areas. The dirt-bag was quite experienced in counter-surveillance techniques and very difficult to follow in daylight hours while on his bicycle or on foot.

Our spin team was also experienced but the team leader got burned by our target after being followed into a corner drug store. The officer drove by one too many times and had his photograph taken when the suspect came out of the store with a disposable camera.

Sammy was also assigned as my investigative partner for a property crime sting operation I put together in the city.

We brought in two undercover operators from the QRP and set them up in our own pawn shop in a high crime neighborhood. Our goal was to find out who was stealing and where they were selling their stolen property.

The Italian Stallion's attention was on the desk and chair he was in and how it was previously occupied by the sole female in our unit, Patty Henderson. She was a looker and Sammy never missed an opportunity to flirt with her when he visited. The Italian version of Burt Reynolds, Sammy caught the eye of many women. Henderson made it clear she wasn't interested; she was married to one of our former Police Chiefs.

"She just left five minutes ago. The chair's still warm if you want to take a sniff."

He hesitated before he spoke, as if considering it. "Norm Strom...you're single and wouldn't understand. Her and I are both married...nothing wrong with a bit of sport fucking."

I flipped my eyebrows. "What brings you into the big city, amigo?"

Sammy swiveled his head from side to side to see who might be within earshot.

I addressed him. "Don't worry, the boss is upstairs and everyone else is either in court or on the road."

"Did you hear about Tony Albano?"

I was not one to seek out gossip and rumors but Sammy always seemed to be plugged in or privy to all sorts of scuttlebutt. "I might have heard his name mentioned." It was my turn to look around to make sure we were alone."

He got wise. "You wanna grab a coffee at Timmies?"

It was a slow day for me and I was catching up on paperwork. "Sure, you buying?" I waited for the excuse; Sammy had a list of them.

"I'm a bit short...the wife raided my wallet this morning. Can you cover me?"

I laughed and we headed out the door on foot. We'd only made it a hundred feet and had to stop for a traffic light.

"So, have you seen Tony around?"

Having heard he'd been questioned by the Queen's Regional Police, I responded. "I hear he's taking some time off...either your guys rattled him or he's messed up over the Gladstone woman. I heard they were dating."

"Yeah, and they were together the night before she got run down. Our guys think the husband knew and couldn't handle it...if he couldn't have her then no one could."

We walked on the sidewalk, headed to the coffee shop. "So, the hubby's a suspect? There's nothing pointing to Tony, is there?"

Sammy shook his head and stepped in front of me to grab the door at Timmies. "The husband looks good for it...they're working on his alibi and the timeline." He followed me inside.

"Are you involved in the investigation? You seem looped in."

We approached the counter and Sammy searched his wallet, as if looking for money. "No, but it's a small detachment and everybody pretty well knows what everyone else is doing."

I let him order his coffee, then I asked for a diet coke and toasted bagel with cream cheese. He pouted and I knew what it meant. "You want a donut or something?"

Sammy smiled. "A peanut butter cookie...if you're buying."

We moved down the counter and grabbed the stuff I paid for. There was a seat in the corner, away from other customers. "So, not that it's any of my business but what else have you got?"

"Did you know the Gladstone family.... when you lived in Cooperville?"

I unwrapped my bagel and took a big bite, answering with my mouth full. "A little, I guess, enough to say hey or carry on a casual conversation. Annie was a hottie, and easy to talk to."

"You never asked her out...weren't you both separated or divorced then?"

"No, I guess Tony beat me to it. Do you really think the ex did it?"

Sammy brushed cookie crumbs from the front of his double-breasted suit. He always dressed like one of the manikins you'd see in the window at a men's formal wear store. "It seems likely at this point...there's no other suspects that I know of."

Chapter Nine

Best Friends

Looking at Sarah and Annie Gladstone, you wouldn't know they were siblings. They had different skin tone, hair color and body style. More than sisters, they were best friends and soulmates. It really didn't matter who was older or younger, with how much they had in common. They did so many things together, like shopping, where they'd go to Costco and split super-sized items in half to share and save money.

They resided on opposite sides of the city so it only made sense to meet in the middle. They visited parks and had picnics, went for ice cream and sampled each other's flavor. The even took night school classes together, aspiring to learn new things and better themselves. At least that's what they told their husbands.

Of course, Sarah knew about Annie's marital troubles. Her sister spilled the beans during more than one tearful exchange. At one point, Annie said she'd been afraid of Dale for months and he was stalking her. There were a few weird and scary incidents, like the time he showed up at the library with flowers for Valentine's Day. The gesture was ironic because Dale thought it was a commercial thing and he'd never given her flowers before.

On another occasion, when she left work, Dale pulled up beside her at a traffic light and asked her to roll the window down. Annie surmised he had been following her and was so scared she called Sarah at work and asked to come visit. She knew better than to think it was a chance meeting and wondered where he might show up next.

When the family was at the hospital, Dale called Sarah's phone and asked what he should do—if he should come there. The police detectives listened in on the call and coached her on what to say. They said to tell him not to come. That is when she became suspicious about Dale's involvement in Annie's death. She wondered if he didn't do it, why would he ask if it was okay to come and why wasn't he already there? He was still her husband and father of her children.

Sarah told police investigators when she received the news of the collision from JJ, she just visited a psychologist who agreed to take Annie on as a client. Being informed how Annie was struck by a car and sent flying through the air, she immediately feared for her sister's well-being. Oddly enough, anger was her first emotion, mistakenly thinking her sister wasn't wearing a seatbelt.

She was driving to work at the time but immediately turned around and called her son. He told her not to worry, that everything would be okay and bad things didn't happen to their family. Sarah doesn't remember any part of the drive to see her sister. She thought many other details from that day were unintentionally blocked from her memory. Sarah was so upset, she was amazed how she made the drive there in one piece.

When Sarah got to the hospital, one of Annie's coworkers was there and explained what had happened out front of the library. Her sister's boss was also there, at Annie's bedside, holding her hand. She was trying to speak and he told her not to. The man has regretted that decision ever since, forever wondering if Annie might have been attempting to tell him who ran her down.

The co-worker said one of the children saw who was driving and described a man who resembled Dale. Sarah's immediate reaction was that she must be wrong because he would never physically harm her sister. Her mind raced, trying to think of someone else who might want to do such a thing. Could it have been someone she was dating? The police had told her Dale had an alibi so it had to be someone else in Annie's life Sarah didn't know about.

Surreal, is how Sarah described feeling when she saw Annie laying helpless and unconscious on a stretcher. She was in the process of being transferred to a hospital in Detroit. Driving there with the rest of her family was another car ride that Sarah did not remember.

Soon, she said everything became all too real, when they arrived in the Motor City and were questioned by QRP investigators. If that wasn't real enough, the doctor told Sarah and her family Annie was a broken woman and he didn't know if she would make it. Sarah wanted to shout out loud. She wanted to know how such a horrible thing could happen.

Annie remained in an induced coma for almost a week. Sarah witnessed the condition her sister was in and couldn't comprehend how she could ever survive such an ordeal. She and her mother remained bedside, crying non-stop. One doctor who came in told them such negativity wasn't allowed and if they couldn't be more positive, they'd have to leave. Sarah came to resent that doctor's remark, feeling it only gave them false hope.

At one point when Marie was holding her daughter's hand, Annie twisted the rings on her mother's fingers, making them think she could hear them and might somehow wake up from the nightmare. Sarah always felt close to her sister and best friend, and wondered how she could possibly live without her.

The big sister thought about her younger sibling, her little quirks and things she loved about her. Not that she didn't have any flaws. If Annie had one, it was that was that she loved too much by the people in her circle and life itself. She was an open person and easily accepted others, no matter who they were. Most of all, Sarah would truly miss her sister's infectious smile.

Sarah and the entire Gladstone family were gathered in a waiting room while Annie had a procedure done to see just how broken she really was. A police detective stood by. She wasn't sure why but didn't think much of it at the time. Sarah chatted with her mom, hoping and feeling everything would be okay. Trying to lighten the mood, they reminisced and laughed about some of Annie's past escapades. A Code Blue was announced over the PA system. Doctors and nurses ran toward her sister's room.

The detective followed them to check on the situation. Within minutes, the doctor came into the waiting room and announced Annie was gone. In her entire life, Sarah had never felt so devastated. She couldn't stop crying and wondered if it was possible to run out of tears. The Gladstone family left the hospital and returned home, knowing Annie would never be with them ever again.

The following days were difficult and blurred for Sarah, having to plan funeral arrangements for the youngest member of their family. It wasn't the natural order of what was supposed to be. What was even more trying for her and the rest of the family was being told not to talk about what police were calling an ongoing murder investigation. It was a big obstacle standing in the way of their grieving process.

With the passing of her sister, Sarah took time off work and didn't feel like getting out of bed. Her loss was immediate and all-encompassing. There would be no more daily phone calls to laugh or cry, no quiet walks in the park, no more ice cream dates where they complained about gaining weight.

Sarah added anger to her list of emotions after Annie's death, especially with the justice system which seemed to have let her sister and family down. The person who everyone thought was Annie's killer, wasn't arrested or charged and he managed to retain custody of her children. The Gladstone's felt *they* were being treated like criminals by the Children's Aid Society, lawyers, and even Dale's parents. To top it all off he never reached out to them or protested his innocence to the family. In their minds, it only went to proving his guilt.

On Sarah's first day back to work, she heard a song on the radio that Annie had talked about during their last conversation, on the night before she was run down. Saddened, Sarah thought her heart would burst. She ran into her office, crying. The song was *Bad Day* by Daniel Powter. Annie said she had a really bad day, on the last day of her life.

Chapter Ten

White Light

Annie Gladstone Daniels was completely lost. As a child she had never been afraid of the dark, but this place was different. At home, when the lights were off, she either knew her way around or simply felt her way into places like the bathroom when she had to get up during the night. But her new surroundings were unfamiliar—no moonlight sneaking through the curtains, no night lights in the hallway. No floors, walls or ceiling. Only empty, dark, space.

Intermittent flashbacks of her past life came into view quickly at first but then slowly disintegrated like a photographic image pix-elating to the point of oblivion. One particular scene was unsettling. A speeding red car. It appeared to have crashed into her but she couldn't remember for sure if it actually took place. But something must have happened to cause her pain and the sensation of flying uncontrollably through the air. Her body felt broken all over.

She saw a light in the distance, like at the end of a long dark tunnel. Annie had heard of the phenomenon before, when people recalled their near-death experience. *Does it mean I'm dying? Is it good or bad to go towards the light? Does it mean life or death?* In her heart Annie felt the light was good and she needed to reach it. If not for her own sake, then for her children's. *Who will look after them?* Certainly not Dale. There'd been a custody battle but he only wanted to keep them so he didn't have to pay child support.

Silence. Darkness. Nothingness, except for what sounded like white noise in the background. Annie thought she heard a faint voice calling to her. Yes, it was her mother asking her to wake up and come back to them. Confusion. *Is mom nearby and cloaked in darkness or is she with the white light?* Frustration. Her brain wasn't processing anything normally. She felt a sense of consciousness, but not really. Nothing made sense.

It wasn't only dark; it was a scary shade of black. She couldn't see the white light anymore. *Where did it go? Is my mom gone too?* How could she possibly find her way out of the void without her mother or the light? Annie wasn't a quitter but heavy gloom weighed her down. As if she was twice her weight and gravity was doing its thing, pulling her deeper into the abyss. Annie had done her best trying to find the light but she was sucked into oblivion.

Part II

The Investigation

Chapter Eleven

Questions

Some of the questions about the vehicle that ran down Annie Daniels were answered when police discovered the abandoned Camaro. It had been stolen shortly before the hit and run. The million-dollar question was who was driving it? According to witnesses at the scene they believed the automobile versus pedestrian collision was no accident. They reported the Camaro had been parked down the road from the library and it appeared the driver was waiting for Annie to cross the street.

To police, it appeared whomever was responsible was aware of Annie's daily routine. But how did they know about the readily available Camaro and its proximity to the library? Was it by chance? That would have to be one lucky coincidence for the suspect and an important detail of their crime left to chance.

Dumping the stolen car immediately after the hit and run meant the driver knew exactly what he'd done and didn't want to be caught by police. If it was simply the case of a thief taking the car for a joyride, the collision would surely have put a damper on their plan. Was it possible the car thief didn't see Annie Daniels and inadvertently ran her down?

Almost immediately after Annie's hospitalization, Dale Daniels became a person of interest in his wife's demise. Information quickly came to light that the couple had separated and were in the process of trying to work out child custody issues. Would any man stoop that far to gain sole custody of his children?

Upon Annie Gladstone's death, Queen's Regional Police classified the hit and run as an attempted murder. At the beginning of many homicide investigations, it's common for the spouse to be at the top of the suspect list. In Annie's case, Dale was the first and only name investigators were able to come up with as a suspect. Nobody had any idea who else could have been responsible.

Information about infidelity, stalking, and even Dale's psychiatric problems leaked and quickly found its way to police investigators. Thinking about and recalling his past behavior, Annie's family and friends started to believe she was killed by her own husband and father of her children. As much as their thoughts leaned in that direction, they couldn't fathom how someone in the family could do such a thing.

Suspect descriptions of the Camaro's driver at the time of the hit and run and when the car was ditched did not match Dale's. According to evidence obtained by police, he apparently had an alibi. At the time of the occurrence, he was captured on video at a nearby gas station.

From earlier sightings, Dale would have been pressed for time to find and steal an available car, locate and run down his wife, switch vehicles, and drive to the gas bar where the time-stamped video supported his being somewhere else at the time of the hit and run. The incident would have to be perfectly planned and executed for him to pull it off. There was no physical proof of that.

Other than Dale Daniels, police investigators had no other potential suspects or leads. They were forced to dig deeper into Dale's story, for proof of his guilt. Even though there was no evidence to the contrary, he remained the only suspect in the death of his estranged wife. Frustrated and somewhat confused, the Gladstone family clung to the hope that someone would be found responsible for Annie's murder.

Even though Dale was not arrested or charged with any criminal offense, he went so far as to hire one of Ontario's top-notch lawyers. He also began to distance himself from the Gladstone family and Annie's circle of friends or co-workers. His actions and apparent lack of concern for his wife's death only reinforced their belief Dale might somehow be responsible. They were left with more questions than answers.

Chapter Twelve

Initial Investigation

Antoine Martineau had been a member of the Queen's Regional Police for over twenty years. Divorced but married to the job, he'd worked in Homicide for five years and Major Crimes before that. He'd covered all the bases as an investigator, receiving extensive training and experience in surveillance, undercover work, search warrants, drugs, firearms, and sex crimes.

The detective chose to pass up a promotion to specialize in homicide and death investigations instead. Known as 'Black Cloud' or 'Doctor Death' by his coworkers, the QRP brass thought Martineau would be a perfect lead investigator for the high profile and brutal murder case of Annie Gladstone Daniels.

Martineau loved the type of challenge a complicated murder investigation could bring. Although his commitment to work had cost him one marriage and perhaps half of his head of fair hair, there was no deterrent to his focus in getting the job done. Physically, he found investigating murder cases worked to keep his weight in check. Long hours, gallons of coffee and stress were his diet plan. Unfortunately, each major investigation took another few years off his life.

While Annie Daniels lay unconscious in a hospital bed, Detective Martineau and a team of investigators tried to piece together the events that led to the hit and run. There was no doubt the red Camaro was stolen but investigators didn't have the heart to charge the owner for leaving his vehicle unattended with the keys in it. As far as he was concerned, the man had done nothing wrong and he didn't appreciate police seizing his car for forensic examination and holding it for weeks.

Witnesses from the scene who were interviewed, agreed the driver of the stolen car appeared to be lying in wait for Annie to cross the road on her way to work at the library. From evidence gathered thus far, police investigators were concerned the hit and run may have been planned by someone who wanted to kill Annie Gladstone Daniels. Unfortunately, none of the witnesses could identify the man who was behind the wheel of the Camaro at the time of the occurrence.

It was the same story at the location where the driver abandoned the Camaro after it struck Annie and left the scene. Witnesses were able to give a description of the man but no identification could be made. Even though Dale Daniels was later suspected as the driver, he did not match descriptions police were given. No other witnesses came forward at that time.

Acting on the information Windsor Police officer Tony Albano dated Annie and spoke to her the night before her death, investigators questioned him and ruled him out as a suspect. He was working at the time of the occurrence and nowhere near the scene.

Annie Gladstone succumbed to her injuries and did not survive the week. She was less than a month away from her thirty-ninth birthday. Her family was devastated at their loss so police investigators kept their distance as much as possible, giving them all time to grieve.

Antoine Martineau and his partner visited Dale Daniels to inform him of his wife's death. They found him at his girlfriend's house. The notification was pre-arranged through the family so detectives could gauge their only suspect's reaction to the tragic news. It's an important step for investigators when dealing with any persons of interest. Their body language and reactions speak volumes to trained and experienced eyes.

When detectives broke the news to Dale he fell to the floor and rolled around, sobbing loudly and uncontrollably. He remained on the floor and wouldn't look at, talk to, or even acknowledge the police presence. Martineau had done several death notifications during his career and he thought Dale's behavior was bizarre. In his opinion it could have been one of two things. Either he honestly and completely lost control of his faculties, or he was acting and auditioning for an academy award.

Two autopsies were conducted on Annie Daniels, the first one in Detroit. The second was back in Canada. She was taken to the Center of Forensic Sciences in Toronto, where victims of series homicides are examined for police services across the province. Experts there concluded that apart from internal injuries and broken bones sustained when struck by a motor vehicle, Annie Gladstone died as a result of her massive head and brain injury.

Chapter Thirteen

The Act of Murder

I went next door to the Provincial Court building to drop off my *Return to a Justice* for a search warrant I had executed at an arson scene. As with all search warrants granted to police, affiants have to report back to the Judge or Justice of the Peace on all things, if any, that were seized during the search. Sammy Fiorino was at the coffee kiosk and waived me over.

"You want a coffee?"

I scoffed. "What, you remembered your wallet today?"

"I raided my wife's purse before work this morning...payback for all the times she's left me empty-handed."

Glancing over at the Justice of the Peace's office, I noted someone else waiting outside the door. "Looks busy this morning."

"Yeah, it's Beauchamp...slowest JP in the city. You ever notice how she reads...line by line, using a ruler?"

I chuckled. "Once. Then she became self-conscious and started making us wait in the hall." I saw a file tucked under his arm. "Shit, are you waiting too?"

He smiled. "Yup, I'm next." Sammy eyed the paperwork in my hand. "Show me yours and I'll show you mine."

"Nothing exciting...a return for an arson warrant I executed at an apartment on Tecumseh Road at Lincoln. The tenant was completely nuts and set his place on fire. He broke every piece of glass in the house, stuffed towels in the toilet and shit on it...then filled the tub with all his clothes and set it on fire."

Sammy flipped his eyebrows. "Really? Was he pissed off at the landlord?"

"Pissed at the world, according to the graffiti he wrote all over the walls in what looked like shaving cream and blood from a cut on his hand."

"Wow...I guess that qualifies him as crazy. How'd you catch him?"

"Wasn't hard...he was smashing furniture and adding it to the fire when the hose jockeys got there."

Sammy laughed. I asked, "And yours?"

He stepped away from the kiosk and swivelled his head from side to side, to see who might be within earshot. "The hit and run in Cooperville."

I scrunched my face, showing my confusion. "I thought you were working in Property Crime?"

Sammy took a sip of coffee. "It's all hands-on deck for this thing...unlimited overtime...whatever it takes." He glanced at the file under his wing. "Search warrant for the husband's car."

"He's still on your hit list?"

"He *is* the list...we've got nothing on anyone else and not enough on him to lay any charges. You know how it is though...only a matter of time before we nail the bastard."

I nodded. "Just like the horsemen...you always get your man?"

We both laughed. I heard the door open at the JP's office. Sammy turned and headed in that direction, dropping his coffee cup into a trash bin on the way. "Catch you later, Norm."

It was then I realized he didn't buy me that coffee. Not surprised, it really didn't matter since I didn't drink the stuff and already had a Diet Pepsi after breakfast. I sat outside the office door, thinking about any past murders I'd personally been involved in. There weren't many. I considered a Forest Glade arson where the husband set the house on fire to kill his wife and almost did himself in during the process.

I remembered an attempt murder from many years earlier when I worked in patrol. Two elderly men were fishing along the Detroit River. They were attacked by two younger men who bashed them on their heads with a rock, tied them in fishing line and threw them in the water so they would drown. Both men were severely injured but miraculously survived.

There was another incident on the east end of the city where my partner and I responded to a stabbing. A young woman was laying naked on the bed, deceased, with several knife wounds to her chest and abdomen. She was my first victim of homicide. Paramedics told us the husband was responsible but he ran from the house shortly after their arrival.

Following directions from the lead detective, my partner and I set up surveillance on a house that belonged to the suspect's parents. After a few hours of sitting in the dark and expecting the worst, the young man showed up and we arrested him at the front door before he could go inside. It was the first and only time I got to utter the words, 'You're under arrest for murder'.

There were other shootings, stabbings, beatings, and arson investigations I was involved in where charges of murder and attempt murder were laid. But I was never a full-time homicide investigator or member of the Major Crimes Unit and that was fine by me. I preferred working on my own and felt I wouldn't fit in with some of the prima donnas or giant egos that worked there.

I noticed a pretty blonde woman walking through the lobby, nearby. My thoughts reverted back to Annie Gladstone and her tragic demise. Having never lost anyone in my own family to such violence, I could only imagine her family's pain. On second thought, no, I could not.

Chapter Fourteen

Digging Up The Past

As in each of the other criminal cases Detective Martineau investigated, he worked them backwards, from the time the crime occurred to a point prior to that, when the seed was planted and began to grow. So far, his investigation revealed Annie's case was not a crime of opportunity. It was planned ahead of time and carried out according to that plan. If Dale Daniels was indeed responsible, some might say it was a crime of passion.

Money is another strong motive for murder and once again some might point to the estranged husband who would retain custody of his children and any cash, insurance or property his wife might own. Besides an ongoing custody battle over the Daniels' children, Martineau had no evidence of a money motivated crime. Accordingly, police investigators had to dig into everyone's previous history. The suspect and the victim.

Police received information in the form of rumors and stories of marital discord from the get-go. Family and friends of the victim casually mentioned it at first, then supplied investigators with statements attesting to those facts. They reported infidelity by Dale Daniels going back at least three years before Annie's death. According to those sources, she was aware of the affair and had confided in her close friends.

One witness Martineau interviewed said Annie found email on their computer confirming her husband was having an affair with another woman that he worked with. Some of the letters were sexually suggestive and Annie confronted Dale about the ongoing infidelity. The lead investigator also received information about physical abuse by Daniels, but nothing substantive that was ever recorded or proven.

A co-worker had reported she saw a large bruise on Annie's arm when she came into work one day. She told the woman Dale had grabbed her by the arm and threw her onto the sofa. Police investigators discovered it happened around the same time Dale had packed his personal belongings and moved to a motel during the separation.

Sometime later the couple spoke about reconciliation and they attended joint counselling sessions. Even with their attempts at holding their marriage together, Dale invented situations where he accused Annie of being unfaithful and trying to sabotage their relationship. This was while he was still involved with another woman.

A family friend told Detective Martineau Dale accused Annie of having an affair with him after a night out with a group of friends. The allegation proved to be false but Dale wouldn't let it go and continued to voice his concern and he knew something happened between the family friend and Annie that night.

It seemed common knowledge to everyone except Annie Daniels her husband was cheating on her. He was often seen by family and friends while in the company of Louise Nantais, a woman he worked with. Annie had her suspicions, of course, but no real proof. Until she found love notes in Dale's back pack he normally took to work with him.

Annie called Nantais directly and confronted the woman in regards to having an affair with her husband. Nantais told Annie not to call her any more. Dale still believed that Annie had a thing with the family friend and the couple continued to struggle with their relationship.

It was during that time Dale became progressively depressed and had a nervous breakdown. Annie being the caring wife and person she was, took him to the hospital where he was examined by a psychiatrist. He continued to visit the doctor and told Annie he was no longer seeing the other woman. He said he wanted to work things out.

A short time later, a family member and a friend saw Dale Daniels with Louise Nantais at two separate public events.

Chapter Fifteen

Dale Daniels

Dale wasn't an overly handsome man, but he possessed a certain charm that allowed him to attract women. Best described as average in height, weight and physique, he was the type of guy who easily blended into a crowd. Although Dale worked as a manual laborer in a factory, he thought of himself as an entrepreneur. In reality, he always wanted to be a rock star.

For police it was a no-brainer, seeing how the deck was stacked against Dale Daniels. But investigators couldn't prove if someone dealt him a shitty hand or he carefully selected the cards on his own. He isolated himself from Annie's family from the time she was in the hospital, something that raised eyebrows and garnered suspicions. Previously considered part of the family, why was he not there grieving with them?

Interviews of family, friends, co-workers, and witnesses painted a picture of Dale as a cheating husband. They pegged him as an unbalanced control freak who went so far as to tell Annie how to cut her hair. His behavior might have gone unnoticed or been ignored by those around him in the past, but every character trait he possessed now came under the scrutiny of police investigators determined to find Annie Gladstone's murderer.

It didn't take a genius to figure out police thought Dale Daniels was more than a person of interest. According to the media and leaked information from the cops themselves, their number one suspect was their only suspect. Out of caution, they obtained a warrant to search his home and seize all his guns, regardless of the fact they were registered and legal.

Perhaps that's why Daniels hired renowned criminal lawyer Richard Morris shortly after police questioned him and before he officially became their number one suspect. Morris was a top gun and one of the most expensive defense counsels in Ontario. Daniels didn't pay a penny in child support to his estranged wife after the couple separated and he cleaned out their joint bank accounts. Perhaps he needed the money to pay his lawyer.

I had my own dealings with Morris in the past, while testifying in criminal court. On one occasion he came into court late, obviously unprepared. Flying by the seat of his pants he cross-examined me, and asked me questions about an off the record conversation we had in the hallway prior to entering the courtroom.

His female law student was in the front row and she almost dropped her brief case when her mentor put me on the spot. Having known the young woman for years, the wannabe lawyer approached me after court and said she couldn't believe what Morris did. The woman admitted she knew Morris was unprepared for the trial but said he was way out of line.

I received a phone call from him a few hours later and he apologized for his actions. He was probably sincere but I think it was more the case he didn't want to piss off the men in blue. There were other questionable cases where I received information about Morris. He allegedly told his clients he could obtain names of police informants for a fee.

Such information, like the identity of police informants, is purposely not entered into police reports for exactly that reason. In some cases, it seemed to me the person arrested was more concerned with who ratted them out, than whether or not they were found guilty of their crime. For the most part, courts at all levels support police investigators in helping to protect the identity of their sources.

In Morris' situation, I had heard things and wondered if his sway over the court had something to do with him being close friends with a local Judge who he happened to vacation with down south. Judges were all lawyers at some point and they all know each other. Many people had suspicions about Morris over the years, wondering about how those who paid him ridiculous amounts of money managed to get off.

Like O.J. Simpson's case, it was magic. Kind of like pulling a rabbit out of a hat. If you stuffed the hat with enough cash, an acquittal would miraculously appear. But for Dale Daniels, no amount of money could keep the heat off him. The deeper police investigators dug, the more dirt they found on him. Unfortunately, it was all circumstantial and not enough to warrant his arrest.

Family, friends, and Annie herself had reported Dale was stalking her and showing up at her work and house uninvited. On one occasion where she found him in her home, he exposed himself and expected sex. He continued telling his estranged wife he wanted her back, although he continued his relationship with Louise Nantais.

In addition to his psychiatric problems, Dale was under another doctor's care for physical ailments. The couple even sought advice from their parish priest, who told Dale to back off. He admitted he'd messed up and done things wrong but was more concerned that Annie had a new male friend. Dale continued to stalk her and on one occasion she found him waiting in her car at the library.

Despite all ongoing efforts to win his wife back Dale Daniels continued with his extra-marital affair.

Chapter Sixteen

The Queen's Cop Shop

I was surprised to see Tony Albano in the Financial Crimes office when I arrived at work. He was fiddling around the desk of recently retired Fraud Detective Mark Ross. The boss walked in behind me and approached Tony with his hand extended. "Welcome to fraud, Tony, glad to have you aboard. I see you're already settling in... I'll leave you to it. Come see me in my office when you're done."

Financial Crimes was on the third floor of police headquarters, the same level as other investigative units like Drug Enforcement, Street Crimes, Sex Crimes, and Major Crimes. Our room was divided down the center by eight cubicles, modular desks surrounded by partial walls about five feet in height. One whole wall was lined with windows, offering a partial view of the Detroit River and skyline.

There was an open area between Albano's new desk and mine, where we kept a long table for laying out active files.

Turning to face me, Tony nodded. "Hey, Norm, how're ya doing?"

I wanted to say 'better than you...I just heard about your girlfriend...what the fuck is up with that'? Instead, I nodded in return and said, "Welcome to fraud."

He gave me a once over. I was dressed in jeans and a golf shirt. "You get to dress like that in here? I thought it was business attire." He waved a hand over his coat, shirt and pants.

"I'm in the middle of an arson investigation and it gets a bit messy at times."

"Don't they give you coveralls?"

"Yeah, I keep some in the van but this cuts down my dry-cleaning costs...they only give us so many cleaning chits. I can wash these clothes on my own...you're single, you know what I mean."

He took off his sport jacket and slipped it over the back of his chair. "We don't have to wear this in here, do we?"

I shook my head. "No, the boss doesn't push it...you only need it to look official in court or for certain high-profile cases. The brass hasn't bitched about our dress code lately so don't worry about it."

Albano looked like a typical cop—short black hair cropped over his ears, regulation moustache trimmed at the corners of the mouth, and an athletic-looking frame. Like me, he was divorced and playing the dating game. Unlike me, he bad-mouthed women all the time, especially his ex-wife. My take was they hated each other and the breakup wasn't amicable.

Being such a bitter man and self-acclaimed woman hater, it made me wonder how he ever attracted any women to date. You can't call all women bitches and then expect them to go out with you. Maybe it was all a show, something he only did in front of the guys.

Tony went about his business and so did I. A half dozen questions about the Annie Gladstone murder ran through my head but I thought better than to ask. Two more of the fraud crew came into the office and welcomed Tony aboard. I remembered when I was unwittingly transferred into the last place I wanted to be and wondered if he'd suffered the same fate. Did it have anything to do with the murder and him being a suspect?

Checking my phone messages, I listened to a call from Denise Gagnier, a young Constable with the Queen's Regional Police. She wanted copies of my reports on a fraud case we worked together but didn't have access to our system. Denise said she was tied to her desk for the day and wondered if I could drop off copies of the paperwork if and when I was out and about.

Always itching for an excuse to get out of the office, I finished checking my messages and email, then grabbed the keys for the arson van. I'm a guy who is always hungry and I considered the hard-boiled egg in my lunch bag that was stashed in the office fridge. An *Egg McMuffin* from MacDonalds sounded much better. Driving across the city, I wheeled through a Mickey D's drive through.

The trip out of the city wasn't bad, heading away from incoming morning traffic. All I had left was half of a diet coke when I pulled into the QRP parking lot. Their weathered old brick building was from a different era, built around the time I was born. Being in civilian attire and not knowing the front desk clerk, I had to badge my way in. Denise Gagnier saw me in the lobby and waved from a back corner of the office.

She stood to greet me and my jaw dropped. I'd never seen her in civvies and she looked pretty damn hot. Her uniform had never revealed the bumps and curves I had only imagined in my perverted old mind. Instinctively, I wiped the corners of my mouth, in case I was drooling.

Denise had wavy blonde hair that tickled her collar, some of it curled under the sides of her face, accenting her cute dimples and high cheekbones. Her perky nose and full lips no doubt drew the envy of other women. Even with only minimal makeup she wore, Denise could have easily graced the pages of any women's fashion magazine.

Trying to maintain eye contact when I got closer, I did my best not to get busted while checking her out from head to toe. Even though I was single and thought '*why the hell not*', she was young enough to be my daughter. To my dismay, she had never given off any vibes to make me think she was at all interested. Denise was all business and I had to respect that.

Normally working as a uniformed patrol officer, I asked if she was on special assignment. Before offering an explanation, she asked what I had in the McDonalds bag. I smile and handed it to her. "I wasn't sure of your diet so I got you an *Egg McMuffin,* Danish and a coffee...I know most cops drink the stuff."

Denise smiled. Her teeth were perfect. "Like you, Norm, I don't drink it. But I'm famished and will take that pastry off your hands." She opened and peered down into the bag, taking a sniff of the Danish before reaching in and pulling it out.

Sammy Fiorino appeared out of nowhere and said he'd take the coffee and egg sandwich off my hands. He scooped the bag off her desk and vanished as quickly as he had appeared. Barely acknowledging my existence, he made sure to check out Denise's ass on his way by.

Gagnier shook her head. "That guy...he's the only Italian I know who never seems to eat at home or bring in any leftovers."

I scoffed. "You ever see his wife?"

She raised her brow in response.

"Picture an olive-skinned, dark-haired beauty pageant queen. She's not the typical Italian Nona you'd find in the kitchen, cooking all day. Her idea of a great Italian meal is one you'd find in an Erie Street restaurant. I think Sammy keeps her around solely as arm candy. She looks way more high maintenance than him, if that's even possible."

Denise snickered. "That says a lot. He is such the typical Italian male...flirts with anything that doesn't have a set of balls."

I nodded in agreement. "So, what are you doing tucked into the back corner of the office and wearing street clothes? Have you been a bad girl?" Dirty thoughts went through my mind as soon as the words crossed my lips.

She smirked. "The Gladstone/Daniels murder...I think everyone in here is working on the case in one way or another. I don't mind. They're kind of abusing me...like a secretary, but I'm learning the inner workings of a major case investigation. It beats doing radar and handing out speeding tickets all day."

I turned to scan the room while Gagnier sank her teeth into her fresh-baked treat. She leaned over the garbage can as not to get crumbs on her paperwork. The room was too small for the number of cops who were crammed into it. Detectives and investigators worked their phones or keyboards on laptops. The electronic hardware was newer than everything else in the office. Furniture resembled the kind of stuff I saw in my grandparents' home when I was a kid.

Not sure exactly how old the police detachment was, I assumed the building was erected around the same time Highway 401 was built, in the late fifties or early sixties. Similar detachments were strategically placed along the four-lane corridor that ran between Windsor and Montreal.

I'd been in the cellblock once, when I worked in patrol, and it looked like something you'd see inside Alcatraz. Windsor's cop shop was no better when I got hired. It had scary places like the underground tunnel that connected the police building to the court house. Even hardened criminals got bug-eyed and looked over their shoulders while traversing the damp, dark and dingy hole in the ground.

Antoine Martineau and I locked eyes for a second when I took in the room. He attempted a silent nod but was distracted by a co-worker trying to get his attention. We'd met at least once before but I couldn't recall when or where.

It was fairly early in the morning but the lead detective appeared stressed and worn out, probably from lack of sleep. Investigators worked up to eighteen hours a day in the early stages of a murder investigation, talking to witnesses and chasing potential leads before they disappeared or dried up.

Martineau's dress shirt was wrinkled and he had the sleeves rolled up. The top button was undone and his loosened tie hung limp like an autumn leaf. I'd had many of those long days when I worked in Narcotics, sometimes going right around the clock. Having some idea what he was going through, I assumed he'd spent the night on a sofa in the Commander's office.

Denise Gagnier worked her tongue around the corners of her mouth trying to catch any icing she may have missed. I couldn't help myself from having naughty thoughts and tried not to stare. She finished cleaning up with a napkin. "Do you know Martineau, Norm?"

"We've met...in a JFO's or party, I think, but I've never worked with him. Looks like he's got his work cut out for him with this murder case."

She raised one eyebrow, kind of how Mr. Spock does it. "They say he's one of our best...the reason he's OIC on this case. It's interesting to watch everything that's going on, and I do want to be a detective one day, but I'm not sure I could handle something as big as this."

The copies of the reports Gagnier wanted were still in my hand. I placed them on the empty corner of her desk where the McDonalds bag had been. "Not everyone is cut out for it, Denise."

"You ever work in Major Crimes or handle a case like this?"

I shrugged. "Too many big egos in that office for me and I prefer to work solo. Like my Arson job...even the boss doesn't know what I do and keeps his distance until he has to fill in the brass or media. I've handled investigations, wire taps and special projects, and I've done crossovers with Major Case on a couple of fatal arsons. Either way, I agree and wouldn't want to be in Martineau's shoes right now."

Denise Gagnier thanked me for the reports and breakfast treat. I smiled, bowed slightly, and found my way out of the dark and gloomy cop shop. If only I was young again, but maybe not so dumb. There were barely a handful of female police officers on the job when I got hired, and only two of those were worth looking at.

Chapter Seventeen

Missing Annie

Marie Gladstone was heartbroken, distraught over losing one of her children, especially the youngest. It wasn't right and if she had to choose, Marie would gladly take her daughter's place. She didn't play favorites but really enjoyed Sundays when Annie helped in the kitchen, prepping meals for the after-church folks who regularly stopped by to talk about the morning sermon or to catch up on local gossip.

Annie liked to pretend she worked on the line in a sandwich factory, carefully lining up slices of bread along the counter, counting them out as she went. Followed by pieces of ham, or scoops of tuna or egg salad, depending on the type of sandwich. She insisted it was the proper way of doing it because that's how they did it on her favorite television food show.

According to those closest to her, Marie wasn't the same person after Annie's death. She withdrew into herself and seemed as though she would never recover from the loss. Her world had become a darker place. As any good mother would do, she wondered what she could have done to prevent such a tragedy. Was it God who took Annie away from her and if so, what did she ever do to deserve it? Surely it was a test of faith.

Joseph Gladstone was a man of few words and he didn't have a lot to say about the hit and run or resulting death of his daughter. As usual, he kept his thoughts to himself, keeping busy with work. He unconsciously compartmentalized such things and secreted his pain in a little box somewhere in the back of his mind. Of course, he felt responsible. After all, it was a father's job to protect his daughter.

Joe senior shared the same thoughts and wanted to say some of the things his family did, but he listened and absorbed it all instead. Usually the family fixer, he had no idea how to repair the damage that had been done. What could he possibly say to his wife and children that would ease their pain? He quietly removed the lid on Annie's box many times in search of an answer. There wasn't one to be found.

Joe junior was more vocal about his feelings, and everything that happened to his sister before and after the murder. Being the big brother, he too felt he could have or should have done more to stop the chain of events leading to his sister's death. Was it a good idea to tell Annie that Dale was cheating on her? He thought so at the time but it didn't seem to change the outcome.

To take pressure off his father, JJ became the family spokesman, trying to keep channels of communication open between police and media. Even though everyone thought Dale killed Annie, he was never arrested or charged with anything. If not his brother-in-law, JJ couldn't imagine who, or why they would do such a horrible thing. He was desperate to find answers for the family, as well as himself.

Sarah missed Annie the most. How couldn't she? They were best friends. They might have been several years apart in age but the sisters grew closer together with age and started having families of their own. Sarah was most upset about Annie's children. Upon her death, Dale took custody and kept them away from the entire family. It wasn't fair to anyone, including the cousins who they'd grown up with.

Sarah tried not to think about everything that led up to the nightmare they had to live every day. Like the others, she wondered if it was her fault and how she could have given her sister better marital advice.

Who would she share her innermost secrets with now? Laugh or cry with on good or bad days? Did Dale really kill Annie? With everything that was being brought to light, it surely seemed that way. Sarah recalled the time Annie actually asked her sister if she thought Dale was capable of killing her. Who could ever know such a thing? If only she had a crystal ball offering insight to the future.

Being the closest in age to Annie, Jimmy Gladstone was terrified at the prospect of never seeing his sister again. Each new day brought feelings of emptiness along with it. Over the weeks and months dealing with Annie's death became a bit less painful but in no way easier. It was like the nagging ache of arthritis, always present and unexpectedly flaring up. He chose to let the criminal case unfold on its own over the next several months...and then years.

The good memories of Annie hurt the most. Close enough in age, they walked to school together and shared some of the same neighborhood friends. They even had their tonsils removed at the same time. Jimmy will never forget recovering in their parents' bed, sucking on popsicles.

They had a juke box in the family store, where he and Annie would play music while cleaning up at closing time. Every time he hears the song's *Hot Rod Lincoln* and *Hold Your Head Up*, he's brought to tears. Growing older they'd hang out in bars and go to rock concerts in Detroit. When they both started their own families, their children played together.

Jimmy concentrated on his own family, rather than let his sister's tragedy take over his life. His father, mother, and siblings each handled Annie's loss in their own way. He thought perhaps he was somewhat like their father and the answer was to bury himself in his work. It helped to mask the pain. If he had a box to hide it in like his father, Jimmy had not found it yet.

The Gladstone's were bombarded with information from friends and coworkers who came forward with their suspicions about Dale. Certain details of the police investigation also made its way to family ears, only adding to their frustration and grief. The more they heard about their son-in-law or brother-in-law, the more they truly believed Dale was responsible for Annie's death.

The one thing particularly odd to the Gladstones, was how Dale had cut off contact with them after Annie's death, even before they had any suspicions of his possible involvement. Taking on the services of a high-profile criminal lawyer before any charges were laid only compounded their ill feelings. To make matters worse, Dale took Annie's children and moved far away, severing all contact with the Gladstone family.

Chapter Eighteen

The Media

During my many years on the job I learned from experience the media could be either helpful or a hindrance during police investigations. It was enough to drive you crazy when they used their police scanners to either beat us to a crime scene or pester us on their arrival before we knew what was going on. In their quest for a Pulitzer or to get the big scoop, it seemed their only mission in life was to get who, what, where, why, and when.

In fairness to all news hounds, I realize they're only doing their job. There are many kinds of reporters and I found the newbies or young and hungry to be the worst. Mostly because they didn't know the right questions to ask, showing their lack of knowledge and experience. Back in my days on the street, newspapers and news agencies had actual investigative reporters who specialized in working the crime beat.

There were certain reporters whose tactics made my skin crawl, asking sensitive questions about victims of crime or trying to get the best angle of someone's loved one, while they lay in a pool of blood. I think we've all heard the mantra once quoted by someone in the news business, "If it bleeds, it leads." It was the truth and I'd seen it first hand on more than one occasion.

There was only one reporter I recall trusting. He worked the crime beat for the Windsor Chronicle and had a knack for knowing how to approach and deal with police officers. We respected each other's work and cops knew he could be trusted to print the truth, with no improvisation or embellishment on his part to sell more newspapers.

As the Windsor Police Service evolved, it became necessary to have a media relations person on hand full time to deal with reporters from various organizations. Some news hounds continued to track down investigators to get the scoop, it was inevitable. But for the most part, we referred them to our media relations officer. They held daily news briefings whenever necessary, to address any current police investigations.

The internet had nearly put news agencies like the Windsor Chronicle out of business, making daily editions of newsprint a rarity. It changed morning routines of people worldwide, who read the paper to catch up on everything from local to world events, sports, the obituaries and even comics. Fingers stained with black ink was considered the norm for those with a daily habit.

To get our attention, news agencies use catchy headlines to snag readers. In Annie's case the Chronicle's front-page headline read, "Cops Say Driver Tried to Kill Librarian," with the byline, "Speeding Car Leaves Woman in Critical Condition." It was not the play on words newspapers normally went for. I appreciated how they kept it real, perhaps out of respect for the Gladstone family.

I pictured Annie in my mind, remembering how attractive and friendly she was. According to the newspaper article, the hit and run vehicle never stopped, and it fled the scene. Police discovered it had been stolen from a nearby variety store and abandoned after the incident. I knew the two reporters who co-wrote the story, and noted how they conducted their own investigation by questioning witnesses and canvassing the victim's neighborhood.

The article went so far as to say Annie and her husband had recently split up. My cop radar keyed in on that. I knew that thirty percent of homicides are committed by someone close to the victim and about thirteen percent are by a family member. In the following days, local and national papers picked up the story and tried to solicit information from the public at the behest of police investigators.

As far as they were concerned, this was a situation where they needed the media to get their message out there. They didn't admit to it at the time but were in desperate need of answers. Police appealed to the public for any witnesses to come forward, hoping to further their investigation. But reporters didn't stop there. They asked JJ Gladstone if the family was aware of any new relationship Annie might have been involved in since her separation.

They also inquired about Annie's relationship with her estranged husband but JJ declined to answer. About a week later the Chronicle reported that Dale Daniels had reached out to them, saying he was offering a cash reward for any information leading to the arrest of the person responsible for his wife's death. He didn't specify an amount and urged potential witnesses to call Crime Stoppers.

Chapter Nineteen

The Alibi

Alibi: *a claim or piece of evidence that one was elsewhere when an act, especially a criminal one, is alleged to have taken place.*

We've all watched movies or cop shows where someone suspected of a particular crime exonerates themselves by proving they couldn't have been responsible for the act because they were somewhere else at the time. In my experience, most criminals are caught in the act while committing 'impulse crime'. If someone with half a brain truly wants to commit the perfect murder, they will need an alibi.

Although Dale Daniels never openly stated or announced to anyone that he didn't kill his wife, he provided a timeline that made it impossible for him to be at the scene of the crime when the hit and run occurred. Then ironically, he publicly announced a cash reward, although he never followed through by specifying the amount of his monetary contribution.

If the man was that concerned about his wife, why did he keep his distance from Annie's family, aunts, uncles and cousins as well as her friends? What kind of father would keep his children away from their grandparents? To create even more friction and doubt within the family, Dale quit his job, packed up the kids, and moved way up north. Joe and Marie Gladstone were devastated and couldn't understand why they weren't allowed to see their own grandchildren.

Dale Daniels had an alibi that put him elsewhere at the time of Annie's death. A time-stamped surveillance video of his image from a local business confirmed it. Investigators viewed the critical piece of evidence and had to agree that Daniels appeared to be somewhere else at the time of his wife's murder. It wasn't the fact video doesn't lie, but police still had concerns about the timeline.

According to statements from Daniels and others who witnessed his movements on the morning of the murder, his day started when he took his son to an early doctor's appointment. Then he dropped off Christopher at home and Annie took both kids to school. The next place anyone saw Dale was at a gas station where he was captured on video.

That is where Dale's alibi became a major hurdle for police investigators trying to prove his involvement. They retraced his steps that morning, actually driving the route at the posted speed limit. Police concluded there wasn't enough time for him to locate and steal the car, get to the library before his wife, run her down, and get to the gas station where his image was captured in his own vehicle.

There were the two citizens who saw the man ditching the stolen Camaro. They supplied police with descriptions that didn't match Dale's. With all the various witness statements, police had a weak circumstantial case at best. In the suspect's defense, the time-stamped video gave him an airtight alibi proving he couldn't have done it. Was Dale smarter than the police and somehow pulled it all off?

Alibi or not, police investigators still had questions. If he was telling the truth and his alibi was rock solid, did he have an accomplice? Descriptions of the vehicle's driver didn't match Dale's. Was he wearing some type of disguise or was it someone else and he is completely innocent?

Chapter Twenty

First Anniversary

The headlines in the morning paper said that it had been a year since the murder of Annie Gladstone and her killer was still at large. As newspapers usually do, they rehashed the whole event of how the poor woman was run down by a hit and run driver in a stolen vehicle. The article went on to say police had no new leads and they were still asking the public for anyone with information to come forward. There was also mention of the Crime Stoppers reward.

From personal experience, I figured if the murder hadn't been solved in a year, it never would. Although, on occasion, someone comes forward with information. Time plays on all our minds and guilt can be a strong emotion that simply gets the best of some, causing them to spill the beans on what they know. Cash rewards can also be a strong incentive. I once had a drug informant who gave up his own brother for fifty bucks so he could buy crack.

I'm sure the Gladstone family was filled with mixed emotions, reading about Annie's death all over again. I can't imagine their pain and what they were still going through. Police surely hoped the anniversary article might jog memories and maybe coax someone in the know to come forward. But surely, it can't be fun to have your family's tragedy recounted by the news media over and over again.

How could it be a year already? I hadn't really thought about Annie's murder case much, having my own arson and fraud investigations to worry about. There was my life in general. I'd been separated for a few years and involved in a couple of short-term relationships. It was difficult searching for the next woman to spend the rest of my life with.

Being alone wasn't a bad thing. Sure, I got lonely but some words of wisdom from my mother before she passed were forever etched in my memory. She told me I had to be happy with myself before I could find someone else to be happy with. A few solo trips between dating and relationships helped me do exactly that. The soul searching paid off and I knew precisely what I was looking for. The challenge was to find it.

A close friend told me I was a good catch. Handsome and well-built, with a full head of hair which was rare at my age. I owned my own home, had a nice car, and a Harley Davidson. Men who visited my house wondered if I was gay, but women loved my taste in traditional decor, a neat and tidy house, and how I could cook. I was to collect a generous monthly pension and was financially secure.

My retirement date was marked on the calendar and I figured my solo trips were a warm-up for what was to come. I had always planned, both financially and mentally, to retire with my pension as soon as I could. After all there was more to life than work. I'd seen too many cops stay far too long for no good reason, because they didn't know what else to do with themselves.

Not me. I made good investments over the years and had no children to support. Granted, my ex-wife took half of everything and the stock markets took a nosedive the year before I pulled the plug. I was young, had my health and big plans to travel the world. If I was lucky enough to meet the next Mrs. Strom along the way, all the better.

Deciding a dose of fresh country air was in order, I took my Harley out for a ride, following the Detroit River west to LaSalle, Amherstburg, and beyond. I cruised by my old house in Cooperville, coming to a stop when I noticed the back yard was different. The new owner had completely ripped out or filled in my ponds and gardens. There was nothing but grass – no more flowers or shrubs, just lawn.

Disappointed, but figuring to each their own, I drove on. Not too far away, I came upon the crossroads where the Gladstone Corner Store stood. My gas tank was near full but my stomach could always use a top up. A young boy was ready at the pumps but I waved him off and parked near the stacks of firewood they had for sale.

I didn't recognize him or the young girl behind the cash register but when I sat down at the lunch counter, Jimmy poked his head out the kitchen window. "Hey, Norm, long time no see."

"I know...I'm just a city slicker now, sorry. I had to stop in for a bucket of your corned beef hash...you still know how to make it the way I like it?"

"You kidding...I flip eggs and chop potatoes in my sleep. Some count sheep, I dream about breaking eggs. How's life in the big city?"

I took a gulp of ice water the counter girl had already slipped in front of me. Seeing I was chatting with Jimmy, she let me be for the moment.

"Same old shit...different day. I'm off today and needed a bike ride to clear my head. Nowhere to ride unobstructed in the big city."

"I hear you. My cousin has a restaurant in Windsor...too many rules and regulations and pain-in-the-ass customers with special diets and food allergies."

I chuckled. Jimmy always told it like it was. "I believe you...now that Elias Deli is gone, I can't think of one restaurant in the city where I can get a decent plate of hash."

He smiled. "How many eggs do you want on top? No toast right...still doing that low carb thing?"

"Yep. I'm just a pain-in-the-ass fussy fart from the city now."

Jimmy laughed and turned to his grill behind the kitchen wall. Standing in waiting, the waitress asked if there was anything else I needed. Jimmy called out, "Her name is Judy...my niece."

I asked for a diet coke. Like always, there was a stack of newspapers at the end of the lunch counter. I grabbed one. It was an issue of the Chronicle, folded to a page with an article on the murder of Annie Gladstone. It was the same story I'd read at home. There was no use in reading it again so I flipped through the following pages to see if there was anything else I'd missed worth looking at.

I don't normally check the obituaries but noticed the memorial for Annie. The clank of a dish on the kitchen counter stole my attention. Jimmy's eyes were locked on mine. I could see the pain in his steely eyes and taut jawline.

He'd added a few new creases to his growing forehead since I'd last seen him. He seemed to know I saw the memorial in the paper and it was as if he was searching for something to say.

Judy put my meal in front of me and asked if I needed anything else. I shook my head. Jimmy pushed through the swinging kitchen doors and pulled up a stool on the opposite side of the counter while I shovelled in my first bite of hash. I savoured the oily and smoked meat flavor while they soaked into the taste buds on my tongue. It's no wonder breakfast was my favorite meal of the day.

Jimmy said he didn't want to disturb my breakfast but he did anyway. His tone had changed and I heard anger in his voice. "A whole fucking year and that asshole is still a free man...acting like nothing happened. He won't let my parents see their own grandchildren. My dad had to take out an ad in the paper to try and track them down...we don't even know where they are."

I swallowed and forked another pile of hash, considering a reply, but Jimmy continued.

"Any idea what the cops have been doing all this time? I know it's not your guys, Norm, but what the fuck? I've lost track of how many times they've told me, 'We're going to arrest him'. Everyone knows Dale did it...he's never even denied it. Wouldn't an innocent person tell the world he didn't do it?"

"I really don't know what's going on, Jimmy. I heard the Queen's finest may have fucked up the investigation but that's only hearsay around my cop shop. You know what they say about opinions."

"They don't tell us shit...well, maybe one guy does...at least he seems to care. Crime Stoppers even did their own re-enactment and added to the reward. The money doesn't matter. Nobody can put it on Dale but everyone says shit about him and we all think he did it. How come the cops can't prove it?"

I shrugged and hoped to take in another mouthful while he continued his rant. Jimmy wiped his hands on his apron, took it off, and fired it through the kitchen window. I felt it was rude to continue stuffing my face so I put down my fork and listened. Jimmy walked over to the cooler, grabbed himself a coke, and sat down across from me.

Besides Judy, there was nobody else in the diner. She made herself scarce when Jimmy started dropping F-bombs. I waited for him to continue. He picked up the paper I'd been reading.

"Nothing but the same old story...played over and over again. Like my family really needs to be reminded. We lived through it...and still are, for Christ's sake."

Thinking I should respond in some way, I replied, "I'm really sorry for your loss, Jimmy. I can only imagine your pain and frustration with the ongoing police investigation. I hate to say it but sometimes these things don't get solved. I've had arson cases where I know who set the fire but couldn't prove it. It sucks but our hands are tied...cops have to play by rules that don't apply to the assholes who commit crime."

Jimmy downed half his coke. I couldn't think of anything else to say so I picked up my fork and broke an egg yolk, letting it ooze over the hash. He stared in my direction but seemed to be looking right through me. His eyes had welled up and I knew he couldn't continue his tirade without breaking down. Jimmy nodded. "Sorry to unload on you, Norm, I know there's nothing you can do about it. Thanks for listening."

Leaving Gladstone's Corner Gas Bar, I climbed on my bike and checked the mirrors while I put my helmet on. Time and age catch up to all of us, me included. Sure, I'd put on some weight over the years and finally lost my baby face in the process. Crow's feet worked at my temples but I still had a full head of brown hair. I felt sorry for Jimmy and wondered how much of his he'd lost in the past year.

Chapter Twenty One

Tony Albano

Mondays are never fun days when you work for a living. For me it meant a backlog of emails and phone messages, and a queue of new cases to investigate. To compound my morning misery, the arson call-in just before midnight on Sunday meant I only got a few hours of rest. I sometimes wondered if the overtime money was worth the loss of beauty sleep. But when I thought about spending that money traveling, it all seemed worthwhile.

I had a phone message from Detroit Receiving Hospital, telling me that one of my fire victims had succumbed to her injuries and passed away. She was an elderly female who lost her husband in the fire that consumed their modest town-home in old Walkerville. It had been almost a week and the case was still under investigation.

The blaze carried over to units on either side, causing severe damage to both, and displacing those families living there. Most people don't understand what it's like to lose everything you own, let alone a family member or loved one. We had a fire in our house when I was a child but our cat woke up my mother. We all managed to get out and the damage was minimal but I'll always remember the kids at school saying I smelled like a burned hot-dog.

Our original determination of cause in the Walkerville house was faulty wiring. Because of the high dollar amount of damage and victim injuries, the Ontario Fire Marshall was called in to take over the investigation. Browsing the file, I wondered if it wouldn't have been better for the old woman to die of smoke inhalation like her husband instead of suffering with third degree burns over most of her body.

Thinking about her pain made me reflect on my previous conversation with Jimmy Gladstone. Not necessarily his suffering, but Annie's. What did she feel when a two-thousand-pound hunk of metal slammed into her? How badly did that hurt? Could she still feel pain after slipping into a coma?

My desk had me sitting with my back to the door. I had to glance over my shoulder to see anyone coming into the Financial Crimes office. On this occasion it was Tony Albano. He stopped in our kitchenette, put his lunch in the small fridge under the counter and grumbled about the moldy fruit left inside. I told him it belonged to Klein; the man never finished his homemade meals and always left them to rot.

Albano cursed and tossed the gooey mess into the garbage can. He made a point of sniffing as he passed by my chair. "Called out to a fire last night?"

I spun my chair around. "Shit. I took a shower and everything...can you still smell it?"

"I hope it's not your cologne...smells like burned hot dogs."

That sounded familiar. I put my nose to my shoulder and sniffed but must have been immune to the odor and couldn't tell. I replied, "At lease it doesn't smell of burnt flesh...that's something that sticks right to your nostril hairs."

Tony unlocked his desk drawers and settled into his chair. "That's good to know...you feel like breakfast this morning? I didn't eat at home and am thinking about a bucket of that hash you like at the deli."

Cops all become desensitized over time with things they see on a daily basis so eating after such a gory discussion was no big deal. I scanned the list of email on my computer and thought about the other things on my to-do list. "I can always eat...got a shitload of stuff to catch up on though."

"Will it still be here when you get back?"

I nodded. "You've got a point. Give me twenty minutes?"

Fifteen minutes later we were out the door and on the way to Elias Deli. Tony wasn't a big talker, who usually stuck with yes or no answers to questions directed at him. But his involvement with Annie Gladstone had me curious, especially after he was a person of interest and questioned by the QRP. He caught me thinking and eyeballing him.

"Go ahead and ask, Norm, you're not the first and I'm sure you won't be the last. Annie told me she knew you...mentioned you used to stop by the lunch counter at her family's gas bar in Cooperville."

I shrugged. "I'm a cop, what'd you expect? How well did you know her?"

"I mostly saw her in a group environment...at the Boar's Head with friends. We got together a few times before Christmas. I knew there was drama with her ex...he'd been in her house and left her stuff for Valentines Day. She asked me what to do and I told her to call a lawyer. You've been dating—you know where to draw the line at getting involved in that shit."

I nodded in agreement and let him continue.

"She came to my place a few times. I was working the day before she was killed and talked to her on the phone. The Queenies interviewed me and I gave them a statement. I never met her ex and didn't care to. It was none of my business."

Tony stopped talking the moment we got to the back door of the deli. It was all he had to say on the matter.

Chapter Twenty Two

Nagging Feelings

Antoine Martineau hated open cases. It was unfinished business—like not eating all the food on his plate—something his mother drilled into him as a child. For the most part, he'd successfully closed the majority of his criminal files. He was a fixer, something else he grew into before police work. It was the type of man he was.

It was his job to investigate crime, find those who were responsible for it, and bring them to justice. He wasn't motivated solely by the steady paycheck. The seasoned detective took his job seriously and not being able to solve a case made him feel like he wasn't doing the job he was paid good money to do.

To Martineau, it was a nagging feeling. Something he felt not only professionally, but deep inside his gut, the place where most of his cop instincts originated. The Annie Gladstone Daniels case tore him apart from the inside out. He wondered if he had given himself an ulcer. No case had ever bothered him like this one. It was an ache he couldn't soothe. A puzzle he was unable to complete because of missing pieces.

The veteran detective couldn't believe it had been a year since her death. A whole 365 days of digging and investigating and interviewing, and nothing but boxes of paperwork to show for it. His gut told him Dale Daniels was responsible. The whole world thought he was the killer. But hunches and feelings didn't make a case. The law says an accused has to be proven guilty beyond a reasonable doubt.

The seasoned detective had no doubts. Neither did his co-workers or the family and friends of Annie Gladstone. How could he make the case against Daniels, slap on handcuffs, and drag him off to jail? Who, what, when, where, why, and how. Martineau had asked himself those questions a thousand times over the past year.

He'd read the anniversary articles in the paper. Martineau received what had become weekly phone calls from JJ Gladstone, checking on the progress of his sister's case. It was so difficult to tell the frustrated man there was nothing new to report on Annie's murder case. He couldn't even lie to give the family false hope; there really *was* nothing new to report.

Detective Martineau opened the initial file, starting at the original call for a hit and run. With nowhere else to look, he thought he'd start from the beginning, going over everything one more time...again. He'd lost track of how many times he'd already gone over each of the reports and statements. That was the job. Maybe he missed something. He could only hope.

Chapter Twenty Three

Bad Coffee

Stale office coffee—it was the best he could muster for the time being. There were no rookies working to do a Timmies run for him. Detective Martineau scanned the mostly deserted investigations office. There were more empty chairs than people. It wasn't like that when the Daniels case was fresh. Almost every detective in the region had been called into action at one point or another.

As in all high-profile murder cases, pressure from the family, media, and upper echelon of the Queen's Regional Police pushed investigators to their limits. As time passed and the flow of information slowed to less than a trickle, manpower was transferred to other cases or back to their original detachments and positions. There was plenty of crime elsewhere to investigate.

Martineau returned to his desk. The solitude was a nice change from the chaos that reigned when the investigation was running full speed and in high gear. Maybe he would find something he missed in the thousands of pages of statements and reports. Having gone over the first responders notes from the scene, the detective brought up the case chronology on his computer screen.

All information submitted was categorized and dated. There were action reports, officer notes, witness statements, follow-up reports, surveillance sheets, search warrants, evidence reports, and tips from anonymous sources like Crime Stoppers. Every single thing that was done by the police was listed in the chronology. It's the Major Case Management system that most large police services use, training all criminal investigators in the same fashion.

I took the course before being promoted to sergeant. It was something our police service taught all potential investigators, thus creating a pool of trained detectives ready to work in various investigative units. It was a good system I later put to use in a major fraud investigation. My acquired organizational skills came in handy when I had to send two banker's boxes of files to the Crown Attorney's office.

Martineau took a sip of coffee. It tasted burnt and bitter but it was hot and loaded with enough caffeine to keep him going for another few hours. He focused on witness statements; those from the scene, just before and immediately after the hit and run. Witnesses' memories were always better when events were fresh in their mind. Memories wane with time.

There were statements from Annie's family, friends and co-workers, along with residents who lived in the area of the library. Martineau considered how much weight to give input from the Gladstone family. It was only natural for them to be biased, but he had to admit their accounting of events prior to Annie's death seemed to be honest and forthright.

Unfortunately, many of their recollections were in hindsight. It was only natural to second-guess oneself and consider the what-ifs or could-haves. It couldn't be clearer to anyone reading statements supplied by Annie's family, they held no grievances against Dale prior to her death. Perhaps with the exception of how he handled the separation from his wife.

According to numerous statements and reports, Dale's behaviour became more and more erratic throughout the marital separation. He continually told Annie he wanted to work on their marriage and get back together, while he continued his extramarital affair with another woman. If there was a common theme in the dozens of statements, it was that Dale Daniels was stalking his estranged wife.

Witness after witness stated how he followed Annie to and from her home and work. He was seen outside both locations, and on a few occasions showed up uninvited and refused to leave when asked. He left her phone messages and email, telling his wife he wanted her back and that he needed to come home. All while he was still seeing his girlfriend.

There were two particular witness statements that Martineau keyed in on. The first was from one of Annie's neighbors who saw Dale three days before she was killed. It was early in the morning and the woman saw Dale driving away from Annie's house in his green SUV. She thought it was strange since she knew the couple was separated.

The second statement was from a woman who lived near the library. She reported seeing a dark colored SUV parked nearby early one morning, before the day of the hit and run. The woman thought it odd since nothing in that area was open that time of day. She had also seen the same vehicle parked there a week earlier. It was the type and color of vehicle Dale Daniels drove. It was parked in the same spot the red Camaro was seen on the day of the crime.

For Martineau, it wasn't hard to deduce that Daniels was stalking his wife, following her movements around town throughout her day. Was it possible Dale had a plan and was practicing how to kill his wife?

Chapter Twenty Four

Search Warrants

Search warrants are an investigative tool police use to obtain potential evidence that hopefully furthers their criminal investigation. In the movies or on television, Judges hand them out like candy on Halloween. In reality, it's a time-consuming and arduous undertaking for police. They say a man's home is his castle and according to our laws, he has the right to privacy within it.

In Canadian law, police must have reasonable grounds to believe a person is committing or is about to commit a criminal offense before they can be physically searched for evidence of that crime. To search a residence, investigators must have grounds to believe that a criminal offense is currently taking place there. Those grounds must be proven or sourced and sworn to before a Justice in an application to obtain a search warrant.

In layman's terms, it means police must give reason(s) why they believe a crime is being or has been committed in a particular place and explain how they came upon that information. If it was received from a third party, police must prove their source is reliable. The affiant (applying officer) also has to submit their investigative background along with any accumulated expertise or qualifications.

I applied for and was granted almost two hundred search warrants during my police career. Most were for narcotics, others for stolen property, some for fraud and arson. I also wrote a couple drug warrants for homicide investigators who were looking for an excuse to enter a potential murder suspect's residence. I wrote a Part VI wiretap warrant once, but that's another story.

The first search warrant written in the Annie Gladstone homicide was to examine the red Camaro that ran her down. Being identified by witnesses as the car which struck her, the Camaro was seized and impounded by police. Fresh damage to the vehicle's front end was consistent with the collision. Even with that, police needed to obtain a search warrant to legally seize any potential evidence they might recover in or on the car.

Though Dale Daniels was a person of interest early in the police investigation, they had no immediate grounds to search his person or his residence. No one was able to put Daniels at the scene of the crime and since it occurred on a highway, there was no reason to believe there would be any evidence of that crime in his place of residence. At the time, there was no evidence whatsoever of any threats by him to harm or kill his wife.

Plenty evidence of harassment and stalking, was found later on Annie's computer. Again, there were no threats but lots of begging and pleading by Dale to take him back and repair their marriage. Even though Annie could not give consent and later passed, a search warrant was obtained to legally retrieve those messages. Legalities such as these have to be considered when it comes to privileged conversation between spouses.

Later, after Dale Daniels became a suspect in his wife's murder, police obtained a search warrant for his telephone records. Police officers cannot obtain those records as easily as we routinely see on television, where pretend cops access everything on their computers with the push of a button. It's the same for financial or banking records. Search warrants are required to gain access to any of those documents.

There were many other search warrants conducted behind the scenes in the Gladstone murder case. One was for the collection of carpet fibers from the Camaro, believed to be transfer evidence from another source. Similar fibers were found in Dale's vehicle but were too common to be called unique and have any evidentiary value in the case.

DNA and latent (fingerprint) evidence were also recovered from the Camaro but anything identifiable belonged to the vehicle's owner. Police investigators also spent hundreds of hours conducting surveillance on Daniels in hopes of recovering castoff-DNA evidence. As investigation into the suspect progressed, detectives obtained more warrants for wire taps and listening devices to install in Dale's home and vehicle.

Chapter Twenty Five

The Polygraph Question

The polygraph test is another investigative tool used by police investigators. I had several tests conducted on persons of interest and suspects in criminal investigations I worked. There are three results that can come from the test: the person is being truthful, they are lying, or the test is inconclusive. Regardless of the results, polygraph evidence is not admissible in Canadian courts.

In polygraphs conducted for my criminal cases, the results were all inconclusive. Watching the tests take place, I really expected more. All questions asked of the person wired to the machine are presented to them ahead of the examination. Knowing all the material in advance, the subject simply has to answer questions with a yes or no response. The machine records changes or spikes in heart rate to determine truths or lies.

Anyone who knows how to search the internet can find various ways to beat a polygraph test. Certain intelligence agencies actually train their people on how to beat the machine. I personally know of one police officer who volunteered to take the test. He lied and still passed. So why do investigators bother to use a lie detector test?

Building a successful criminal case is all about obtaining information by any means possible. Generally, people like to talk. In many cases when they're being interviewed or interrogated, they say too much and give investigators ammunition to further their case. Such is the case with polygraphs, where the test allows for a whole new line of conversation and questioning.

I've sat behind one-way glass watching my suspects while they were polygraphed. Even though the questions are preselected, the person in the hot seat still has certain physical reactions and body language that sometimes gives them away. It's almost like a game of truth or dare, making the decision to take the test.

If accused of a crime, should you volunteer to take the test or agree to one when asked? I believe it depends on whether or not you are guilty or innocent. In my experience, most innocent people jump at the chance to take the test. In some cases, it's to get investigators off their back and have someone believe them. They really have nothing to lose if they are truly innocent.

It's a different story for guilty people, even if they think they can beat the lie detector test. Knowing it's not admissible in court should be the clincher but there's always a fear of being discovered. Failing might just be another nail in their coffin.

Dale Daniels was offered the chance to take a polygraph to prove his innocence in Annie's murder. He declined.

Chapter Twenty Six

Coping

During the months and then years after Annie's death, the Gladstone family continued to struggle with their grief and loss. Joe Junior tried to stay abreast of the police investigation but each and every phone call found they were no closer to finding and arresting the person responsible for Annie's murder. The return calls became more infrequent, by investigators who seemed less interested.

The family received lots of support from friends and the community as a whole, who went so far as to put on fundraisers, adding reward money to Crime Stoppers coffers. But anniversary announcements in the news media faded with time, while Annie's killer remained at large. For the general public, Annie Gladstone's demise had become just another sad story.

The Queen's Regional Police, Crime Stoppers and Gladstone family continually bumped up cash reward offers for any information that would lead to an arrest of whomever was responsible for Annie's murder. Oddly, Dale Daniels never specified an amount for the reward he said he was offering and his statement was lost in newspaper recycle bins.

The community also planted a commemorative tree in front of the library where Annie took her last steps. It is marked by a plaque that honors her memory. Thoughtful as all these events were, it only reminded the Gladstone family of their loss and the pain they continued to suffer. Could catching and bringing her killer to justice ever ease their pain or give them any closure?

For the family it was a long and drawn-out investigation, where it was difficult not to give up hope anyone would ever be charged for the crime. It affected each and every one of them negatively. Annie had been very close to her children but her family lost them as well. After Dale moved away with his son and daughter, none of the Gladstones were allowed any contact with Christopher or Ashley.

They eventually came to their own conclusions who may or may not have killed Annie. Everyone else believed Dale was responsible. How did he ever explain everything going on to his children? What, exactly, did they think? Were they brainwashed by their father to make them believe he was innocent? Is that the reason he wouldn't let them have any contact with their relatives? Was he afraid they might hear another side of the story?

There was no doubt in Jimmy Gladstone's mind that his onetime friend and ex-brother-in-law killed his sister. To him, all evidence said it was so. He'd seen and heard too much. If not Dale, then who on earth would want to kill Annie? Did the bastard hire a hit-man or was it one of his buddies? No, Jimmy was sure it was him. He was a coward who couldn't have her to himself, so he made sure nobody else would?

Chapter Twenty Seven

Undercover Operations

I was never officially trained or certified as a police under-cover operator but I was involved in several undercover pro-jects and investigations, and made a few drug buys. It takes a certain type of person—like an actor, to take on a different persona to blend in with the criminal element in certain sub-cultures. Not all police officers are cut out for such work.

Certain officers look and act like 'cops' because of their training and the demeanor acquired over years of doing the job. It takes skill and determination to ignore those traits and become a successful undercover operator. For some U/C op-erations, officers have to 'go under' for months at a time. In certain cases, it can affect their personality and have detri-mental effects on their personal or family life.

For me, making an undercover drug buy wasn't a big deal. During my time in narcotics I let my hair grow, put on some weight, and dressed in street clothes. I had some experience with buying and selling drugs as a teenager, prior to getting hired by the police force. It was part of growing up. Having that knowledge gave me an advantage over officers who knew nothing about drugs prior to becoming a cop.

Whether it's a simple drug buy, a jail cell insertion or full-blown criminal investigation, an operational plan must be put in place before anything can move forward. An undercover operator suited to the particular situation has to be selected and briefed. With any U/C officer, a 'handler' must be assigned. Someone who can watch, guide and oversee everything the undercover cop does in that capacity.

The handler's job can be taxing, trying to keep tabs on and control of the U/C, who can be out of sight for hours or even days on end while submersed in a criminal environment. Sometimes safe houses are used—a place where the U/C, hander, and other investigators can surreptitiously meet without compromising the operator's true identity.

In the Gladstone/Daniels murder case, police used various undercover initiatives in an attempt to gather potential evidence and build a case against the estranged husband. These types of operations have to be kept secret and conducted without the knowledge of the victim's family or news media. In most cases police officers not directly involved in the investigation are also kept in the dark.

Conducting such operations in secrecy is done to protect the undercover operator as well as the integrity of the investigation. There were times when the Gladstone family was all over the QRP for their lack of action. Detective Martineau truly felt for them but he couldn't reveal any undercover operations that might have been going on at any given time.

Anyone who watches police shows or movies may have seen instances where police insert an undercover operator into a jail cell with the accused, hoping they might spill the beans and confess to their crime. This is perfectly legal and I have personally seen it done for police investigations I was involved in. Some criminals can't keep their mouths shut and like to brag, so it does work at times.

With no new leads or information to incriminate Dale Daniels, the QRP got warrants to bug his vehicle and home. For police to obtain warrants to intercept private communications, the bar is set much higher than normal. Beyond that, they have to surreptitiously enter the targeted vehicle or residence to insert listening devices. In this case, it meant stealing the suspect's vehicle and physically breaking into his house without his knowledge.

Investigators were unable to get anything from the bug in Dale's vehicle. Since Daniels spent most of his time at home alone, Detective Martineau reached out to his girlfriend. He approached Louise Nantais and got her fired up by asking a lot of pointed questions about the hit and run. The plan almost worked.

Subsequently, Nantais went directly to Dale's house and told him all about the police harassment. Investigators overheard the beginning of their conversation as they carried on about the murder, near the listening device. But unfortunately, they took the conversation into another room where the bug could not clearly pick anything up that was said.

Police also inserted an undercover operator into their investigation, with the intent to get close to Daniels. They had been conducting surveillance on him and knew all about his habits and daily routine. Logistics became a problem after Dale moved north but the QRP managed to get their U/C into his small circle, and hoped he might talk about his ex-wife's murder.

Dale had used his savings, a partial pension buyout from his previous job, and whatever he raided from their joint bank accounts to purchase a lube shop franchise. Having no personal experience in running his own business, Dale counted on the turnkey operation to run itself. When he advertised for employees, it presented the police with a perfect opportunity.

Undercover police officer Stan Acovski applied for the job and told Daniels he was new in town, having previous experience working in an auto repair shop out west. The U/C was a car buff who like to tinker with his own car's engine so it made Acovski's cover story more believable. For their own protection, it's always better for U/C operators to stay as close to the truth as possible so they don't get caught up in their own lies.

Dale hired Acovski as his first official employee and became convinced of his role when the U\C trained the next man he hired. Daniels kept his distance at first but later warmed up to Acovski over lunch one day. The U/C received a staged phone call in Dale's presence, from his estranged ex-wife demanding child support. Police investigators thought it would only be a matter of time before Daniels confessed his sins to his new friend.

All good plans are never foolproof. After only a few weeks working at Dale's lube shop, Acovski got a real call from home with bad news. His twin brother had been killed in a motorcycle accident. Stan had to extricate himself from the investigation so he could attend to funeral arrangements and look after his sister-in-law and niece. The family tragedy kept him from returning to the investigation.

Chapter Twenty Eight

Alternative Theories

It wasn't like the police and Detective Martineau didn't look at other possibilities for who could have murdered Annie Gladstone. Although no other suspects or even persons of interest came to light, as an accomplished and experienced investigator Martineau knew he had to consider alternative theories. There were a few that came up.

Even though he was casually dating Annie, Tony Albano was ruled out almost immediately as a person of interest. If Annie was dating or had seen anyone else who might have had a problem with her, no names were ever put forward. There was the friend of the family that Daniels believed she had an affair with but both he and Annie vehemently denied it and nobody else could back up Dale's belief.

Someone suggested that Daniels might have hired a hitman to carry out the murder of his estranged wife. If true it could have gone a long way to helping put Dale somewhere else at the time, as proven by his alibi. Again, there was no physical evidence to suggest he hired anyone to carry out the deed.

It was also put forward that one of Dale's friends could have helped him or even been solely responsible and drove the car that struck Annie. Other than family, his girlfriend and a few co-workers, Daniels really didn't have any friends...especially any who would agree to murder his wife.

Detective Martineau also had to consider the car thief was someone else and that person accidentally ran down Annie Gladstone. If that was the case, there was no logical reason for the vehicle to be parked and idling in the empty lot near the library just before Annie was struck. It could make sense the driver panicked and fled the scene if he unintentionally hit someone. That happens all the time.

In a case like this identity is an issue. No witnesses ever came forward to positively identify Daniels as being the driver of the stolen car at the time of the incident or when it was abandoned a short distance away. However, the image of him captured on video at the time Annie was run down supported his alibi and left police investigators with zero evidence against him.

As far as alternative theories go, Martineau struck out on all accounts. Even though he had no actual proof that Daniels committed the heinous crime; the detective firmly believed he was the man responsible for Annie Gladstone's death.

Chapter Twenty Nine

Meeting Martineau

Out of the blue one day, I received a phone call at work from QRP Detective Antoine Martineau. He said he was glad to catch me in the office since he heard I was about to retire. The regional cop was correct, I had less than a week left on the job and was mostly desk-bound, concluding any cases I could and passing on others I couldn't.

Martineau asked if I had time for a coffee—we could meet at the Timmies on Manning Road. He said he'd rather meet and talk in person. I was immediately curious and wondered if it had anything to do with Annie Gladstone's murder case. Always looking for an excuse to get out of the office, I agreed on a time to meet him.

After waiting twenty minutes and wondering if the QRP cop was a no-show, I checked my phone for his number and called him. He laughed and said it had happened to him before. There was more than one Tim Hortons on Manning Road and we each went to a different one. After clearing up which location I was at, Martineau said he'd come to me.

Inside the coffee shop and upon recognizing each other, we smiled and exchanged a handshake. He chuckled. "Who'd of thought two detectives couldn't find the right Timmies...there's only three of them on this stretch of road."

The lead investigator on Annie's case looked more relaxed than the last time I'd seen him. His suit appeared fresh off the rack but his demeanor still gave away a tired soldier. Martineau asked if I wanted something before heading to the counter. Brushing leftover bagel crumbs from the table, I shook my head. He returned to the seat across from me with a coffee and pastry.

I lifted my chin in the direction of his breakfast treat. "Bit of a sweet tooth?"

"My weakness. I blame it on my French heritage...but I really didn't get into pastries until we visited Paris. They eat chocolate croissants for breakfast...have you been there?"

"Twice, actually. A bus tour the first time and we stayed for three days on our own the second time. I enjoyed seeking out different neighborhoods and Versailles always blows me away. We took in all the major tourist attractions, of course. Renting a car and driving out of Paris was crazy but touring the chateaus in the Loire Valley was amazing."

Martineau took his suit jacket off and slipped it over the back of his chair while I filled him in about the trip to France. "Wow, I heard you liked to travel...you sound like a pro. Any post retirement plans?"

I took a swallow of my pop. "Yup, I'm outa here in seven days...Cambodia, Vietnam and Thailand. I have a buddy in Phnom Penh who's going to help me acclimatize to Southeast Asia."

Martineau had his teeth into the pastry. Flakes fell from his lower lip when he answered. "Holy cow, you *are* a serious traveler." He flipped his tie over his shoulder to avoid spilling anything on it. Sign of an experienced cop.

It appeared he had more to say on the topic but I interjected while he took advantage of the dessert he was enjoying. "Sounds like you did your research on me. I know we've seen each other in passing over the years or maybe worked from different sides on a joint force operation?"

He held up a finger while he washed his last bite down with coffee. Nodded in agreement. "I talked with one of our drug guys who spoke highly of you...says you did a sting operation he was involved in...ran your own pawn shop?"

I scoffed. "Yeah, we gave it our best shot. As usual the bean counters put an early end to it in order to satisfy their budget requirements. Fighting crime is expensive...don't you know?"

Martineau guffawed and nodded. "He also mentioned you're the guy to talk to about police informants...that you have a revolving stable of them. More than any other cop he knows."

I shrugged. "I've handed most of them off to other investigators now that I'm pulling the plug. Does this have something to do with the Annie Gladstone murder? I heard you're the lead on it."

Martineau slowly lifted and lowered his head in silence, as if formulating his next words. "Yeah, it's all mine...the best and worst case of my career. One that has no end in sight. I heard you knew her...from when you lived in Cooperville?"

I flipped my eyebrows. "You hear a lot...must be a good detective."

He offered a flat grin. "I try, Norm. I don't know what you might have heard but we're looking hard at the ex-husband.

Problem is we can't build enough of a case to lay any charges on the prick. Our latest U/C play came to a crashing halt." He leaned in closer and locked eyes with me. "That's where you come in."

Matching his posture, I flicked my eyes left and right to see who might be within earshot. "How exactly can this retiring traveling cop help you?"

Martineau checked from side to side, mimicking me before continuing. "I...we're hoping you might have an informant or an agent we can use and insert into our investigation. We already put someone close to Daniels but the poor bastard had to bail because of a death in his family."

I listened intently while he gave me more details, and wondered who I might know who'd be able to fit the role or pull it off.

"Anyone come to mind...who we might be able to sign up and put into play?"

Chapter Thirty

Here's Johnny

Police agents and police informants are two different animals. I had lots of informants from all walks of life who supplied me with information for various reasons. It is always important to know their motivation. Reasons include money, eliminating dealer competition, revenge, civic duty, and pretending to be a cop or spy.

Police informants supply information anonymously and their identities are kept confidential for their own safety. Investigators cannot ask or specifically direct informants to perform certain tasks to gather information. Doing so would make them an agent and they would have to testify in open court. Informants can be paid in cash or receive consideration on outstanding charges as compensation for information provided.

On the other hand, police agents can be solicited or directed by investigators to carry out specific tasks. They sign a contract with a police service and are paid an agreed upon amount, usually monthly, for their services. At the conclusion of the investigation, agents are expected to show up for and testify in court. On occasion, some have to be relocated for their own safety.

When asked by the regional cop, I had a few names in mind but my thoughts had been on retirement for the past year and not on old informants. I'd lost track of two but had heard that one was still in play. I eyed the QRP detective deadpan and said, "Here's Johnny."

Antoine Martineau scrunched his face and looked around as if I'd just announced someone's arrival. "Wha...who?"

I laughed. "Here's Johnny. That's what we called him—he's a piece of work but usually got the job done. I met him when he worked for the Mounties, who paid him well. He liked hanging out with the guys in my narcotics unit better and he'd show up every so often to pitch us a play on a drug dealer he'd gotten close to."

He always referred to himself in the third person like, 'Johnny knows a guy dealing pounds of weed' or 'how much can Johnny get paid for this crack dealer'? His real name is Jake Wilson but he preferred us calling him Jokester because we all had cool monikers and he thought of himself as a funny guy. He took nothing serious, no matter how dangerous the gig might be."

Martineau nodded along. "Here's Johnny." He guffawed. "Sounds like the kind of guy we can use. Any idea where he is or how to get in touch with him?"

I finished the last of my diet coke. "Not a clue. Last I heard he was up north somewhere, trying to help clean up a meth problem. He might still be registered with the Horsemen...he'd talk them into long term contracts and then hit up smaller cop shops for extra money on the side. He's a scammer for sure...and a big bull-shitter. Likes to let everyone know just how great he is."

The homicide detective listened and had taken to jotting a few things down in his notebook. He wrote down the Mountie's name I suggested to get in touch with while filling me in on the role he wanted him to play. I laughed to myself, picturing the James Bond wannabe in a grease pit doing oil changes. Give him a week on the job and he'd be telling people he owned the place.

Martineau changed the subject back to Annie Gladstone and asked how well I knew her. He slouched in his chair and seemed somewhat more relaxed, as if he'd just solved the daily Wordle puzzle and was able to get on with his day. I filled him in on what I knew about Annie and couldn't resist dropping Tony Albano's name.

The seasoned detective only offered a flat smile and slight turn of his head, telling me without words he wasn't at liberty to get into it. I could appreciate that. It was a high-profile murder case and the intimate details were really none of my business. To change the subject, I asked how far away he was from retirement.

Antoine said he had some family issues to deal with before he could even think about a date to pull the plug. I could tell there was a lot more to that story but the murder case was his top priority and he wanted to see it through. He eyed the bottom of his empty coffee cup and got up from the table. After slipping back into his suit coat, he offered his hand and thanked me for my time.

I got up and wished him luck before we went our separate ways.

Chapter Thirty One

Traveling

I was almost a year into retirement when I received a subpoena to attend court for one of my arson investigations. As a newborn civilian, I wasn't thrilled about the request for two reasons: I would only receive a small stipend that wouldn't even cover my parking for the day, and there was a problem with the court date. I planned on being in South America.

When I tried to solve my dilemma with a simple phone call, the clerk in the Crown Attorney's office told me the man I needed to speak to would be tied up in court all day. I knew leaving a phone message for Randall James wouldn't be enough to get excused from my court appearance so I made a trip downtown to the Provincial Court building.

From past experience, I knew the best time to catch an Assistant Crown Attorney was to wait for them outside of the courtroom they were scheduled to be in that day. Upon entering the court building I learned what it was like to be a civilian. They stopped me at the security check point just inside the front doors. I was about to be frisked by the young officer when one of the veterans recognized me and waved me through.

He was busy talking to someone else so I nodded and mouthed the words, 'thank you'. I saw a lawyer I knew in the elevator. We had worked together many years earlier when he was a cop. A high-speed chase we were involved in flashed through my mind. Seeing his smile, I assumed we shared the same thought for a second. His phone rang and he got off on the next floor before we had a chance to catch up.

The hallway was pretty well empty when I approached courtroom number eleven. Most cops don't show up until the last minute, just before court is scheduled to start. The criminals are always easy to spot, wearing clothes that appeared slept in. They rarely showed up for court on time. It's quite normal to see panicked lawyers on their phones, trying to get their clients to court.

The security officer and I recognized one another but neither of us remembered the other's name. He was sitting outside the courtroom door, which was still locked. I peeked through the window and saw a clerk organizing her work. Out of courtesy, I told the court officer I was waiting for the Crown. He nodded more with his eyes than head, as if he was about to fall asleep.

As time passed, more people gathered in the hall outside the courtrooms. Like me, they took turns peeping through the window and pulling on the locked door handle. About ten minutes before court was scheduled to start, I recognized Randal James charging toward number eleven. He was oblivious to everyone around him and I knew his mind was on the stack of files tucked under one arm.

He was a newer Assistant Crown, who'd started about five years before I retired. He didn't recognize me and walked past before entering the courtroom. I followed him inside right up to his table, where he wasted no time laying out the files that would fill his day. Inserting myself into his life, I quickly introduced myself and gave him the Cole's Notes about my case and problem with attending court.

In my second breath I offered him a solution. I explained how I was training my replacement at the time and he could testify to everything, same as me. He paused in thought while facts in a dozen other cases passed through his mind. Without ever making eye contact, he told me to relay the message to his office and have the other officer subpoenaed in my place. A defense lawyer already had his other ear so I said thanks and left.

I pushed the courtroom door open at the same time Antoine Martineau was reaching for the outside handle. He pulled his hand back just in time to save his fingers from being crunched. The detective wore a look of surprise on his face. "Norm Strom, I thought you'd be off traveling the world, somewhere."

"I'm between trips...here trying to quash a subpoena so I can go on my next adventure. Did you know they only pay eight bucks for a court appearance when you're a civilian? What a joke...no wonder people don't want to get involved and come here."

Martineau turned around and we continued our conversation in the hallway. It had only been about twelve months but the veteran detective looked at least five years older. I took consolation in the fact that I got out while I still had my health and the job hadn't gotten the best of me.

"I hear you, Norm. It's good to see you...where to next?"

"South America...Peru, Chile, and Argentina—the trip's more important to me than some nut-bar who torched his own apartment."

His thoughts seemed to be elsewhere. I hadn't heard anything about the murder case over the last year and had to ask. "Hey, what ever happened with the Annie Gladstone case...did you nail the asshole?"

Martineau's chin dropped to his chest. He looked defeated. "No. He's still out there and we've got fuck-all on him. This case is going to be the death of me. I'm afraid to talk to the family anymore...there's nothing I can tell them to give them any sort of closure." He shook his head in disbelief.

"Wow, that's unreal. Hey, how did Here's Johnny work out?"

He scoffed. "Accepting a phone call recommendation from our previous undercover operator who'd worked for Daniels, he hired Here's Johnny to replace him. But he never really warmed up to the new guy. I travelled up there and tried to heat things up by casually bumping into him at a gas station. I got in his face and asked why he wouldn't take the polygraph to protest his innocence.

It didn't go well. He didn't say shit and laid off Here's Johnny shortly after that. I gotta tell you, Norm, Daniels is either really smart or the luckiest fucker around. I'm sure his lawyer had something to do with it...we heard Morris warned him not to make any new friends."

"It surely sounds like he's got a horseshoe up his ass. You guys really went all out."

"That's not the half of it...we spent hundreds of hours following the prick and grabbed some DNA castoffs for good measure but we still came up empty handed. It's been the case from hell for me. I'm meeting with the Crown again today for our monthly progress report. We keep adding tidbits of potential evidence to see if we can arrest and charge the fucker."

Martineau looked back over his shoulder when someone came out of the courtroom. "Maybe I'll catch you later, Norm, over cocktails? I'd like to hear about the trip...gotta go."

Chapter Thirty Two

Annie's Kids

Sadly, it's children who get caught in the middle of domestic disputes and family breakups. I'd seen it firsthand too many times on the job. Parents screaming at each other, physical assaults and worse. At one call I attended, the parents were out on the street—each one of them with an arm, trying to pull the little boy in two different directions. A human tug-of-war that undoubtedly left the child scarred for life.

The worst domestic I saw was on a Christmas Eve when a woman's new boyfriend got into it with her ex-boyfriend. Drunk and with the seasonal blues, he came over to belittle the new guy and spread his holiday cheer by tormenting his ex one more time before the new year. Taunts and insults turned into a fistfight between the two men.

Instead of taking it outside, they went at it in the living room. They shared the small space with a fully-decorated Christmas tree and all the children's neatly wrapped presents. I'd seen the aftermath of many trashed homes and barrooms left in ruins by combatants who's only concern was beating the crap out of their opponent. This was different.

It was Christmas, a time of peace and joy and family. With little respect for the home of the woman they both had feelings for, the two men wrecked the place. I saw no evidence of the Christmas spirit when I walked into that room. The tree, with all its colored bulbs and lights and tinsel, was smashed into a corner as if run over by a truck.

Presents with festive wrapping were crushed and spattered with blood. I'd seen murder scenes that weren't as disturbing. Both men were covered in each other's blood, the current boyfriend being attended to by paramedics for knife wounds he received during the altercation. They patched him up and carted him off on a stretcher. We took the ex-boyfriend away in handcuffs. Sadly, the woman's young children witnessed the whole thing.

Back at the police station, writing up our reports, we noticed one of the attending officers was absent. His partner told us he had an important errand to run. Odd, I thought, since it was now after midnight, Christmas morning. We only found out later that the patrol officer woke up the owner of a toy store and returned to the home with gifts for the children so they would have something to open when they got up in the morning.

After leaving the court building and seeing young children waiting outside for their parents, I wondered how Annie's kids fared during their family ordeal. How did they cope with having their mother murdered and father suspected of doing the deed? Did they ever take sides or come to their own conclusions as to what really happened?

In a state of denial, while trying to cope with her mother's death, Ashley once said maybe her mother really wasn't dead. Christopher asked if he would have been old enough, could he have visited his mom when she was in the hospital. Rightfully, they were both upset and scared. They even wondered if the murderer would come after them. Their whole world had been torn apart.

The children had always been close to the rest of the Gladstone family, often visiting and sleeping over at their grandparents' house. In the morning they'd all go to the family store and have breakfast together. Christopher loved to service customers at the gas pumps, helping his uncles by cleaning windshields and putting air in tires. Ashley mostly got in the way in the kitchen.

They had both grown old enough to know what was going on. Did they feel isolated when their father moved them so far away from the rest of their immediate family? Annie's parents had reached out, hoping to at least talk to them, but weren't even aware of where they were living. JJ had to put an ad in the paper, trying to reach his own blood. Did the children know their aunts and uncles and grandparents were looking for them?

It took JJ a few years to track them down. He begged Dale to at least allow the children's grandparents to talk to them. Daniels said he wasn't on speaking terms with his in-laws. They tried driving for hours to visit the kids but had to resort to putting an ad in the local newspaper to wish them Merry Christmas and Happy Easter. That first holiday without Annie and her children was the most difficult, not all being together as in previous years.

Sarah felt she was letting her sister down; she had promised Annie she'd always ensure the safety and well-being of her children. At first, she thought the family received a small reprieve when Children's Aid granted Jimmy and his wife visitation rights. But those visits had to be supervised and her niece and nephew weren't allowed to spend time with their cousins or the rest of the Gladstone clan on holidays.

It's not like Christopher and Ashley couldn't read or weren't aware of what was repeated year after year in the newspapers and media. Or that other kids didn't find out who they were and subjected them to unwanted criticisms and uninformed opinions. We've all been there and know how ignorant people can torment each other, whether it's ill-intended or not.

The Gladstone family suffered for years, losing Annie and her children. One day Joe and Marie got a call from Christopher. He said he wasn't getting along with his dad and wanted to know if he could move in with them. There were no reasons given and none were needed or asked. Christopher Daniels returned to Cooperville and moved in with his maternal grandparents.

Ashley stayed and put up with her father. Again, no reasons were given and none were expected. Maybe she believed her dad couldn't possibly have killed her mother and was completely innocent of the crime for which he was suspected. Perhaps she was gullible and been brainwashed into believing everything her father told her. Perhaps she and Christopher had different opinions on the matter.

Regardless of whom they decided to live with, the death of their mother would always weigh heavy on them. Whether it really was their father or a yet un-named man who murdered her, that person had not answered for their crime and was still at large. How does anyone deal with something like that?

Part III

The Injustice System

Chapter Thirty Three

The Arraignment

The Gladstone family was shocked when they received news of Dale's arrest. It had been seven years since Annie was killed. Why now? Was it a sign of bad luck the investigation took that long and the powers that be decided it couldn't wait another seven years? Had some new piece of evidence come to light? Did Daniels finally break down and confess?

As usual, police kept family in the dark and they had to attend Dale's arraignment to find out what was going on. Joseph Junior searched the courtroom's front pews for cops he knew but didn't see any familiar faces. The weekly phone calls to and from Detective Martineau had stopped long ago. He was told the case's lead investigator had retired and moved north to work in the family business.

A balding man, dressed in a black suit, was sitting in the front row. He glanced over his shoulder and nodded. JJ wasn't sure but thought he might be a detective with the QRP. Maybe he'd met him over the years, there were so many of them involved in the investigation. Time blurred their faces and his memory of everyone except for one man seated at a table up front...Dale Daniels.

Marie leaned in and asked her eldest son where the nice detective was, the one that seemed so concerned and had treated them well. Maybe he could tell them what was going on. JJ searched the courtroom again, worried that he didn't know anyone and thinking Martineau would show up for something like this after all the time he put into it. The suited man with greasy-looking black hair seated beside Dale looked familiar. A lawyer for sure, someone Joe Junior thought he recognized from the newspaper.

JJ swiveled his head from left to right, checking on his parents and siblings and their spouses. The Gladstone family filled three pews. They all wore the same face, a solemn stare showing years of pain and frustration. Perhaps it was shell-shock from the sudden arrest or bewilderment at what was about to transpire. Jimmy was at the end of the row, squirming in his seat.

With aisle access, JJ thought his younger brother chose his seat with a quick exit in mind. The elder watched for a few seconds, wondering if Jimmy would bolt or charge the front of the courtroom and beat the shit out of Dale. JJ grinned at the thought and turned back to his ex-brother-in-law. Maybe it was the kind of justice his family needed for peace of mind. The asshole just sat there, gazing in the direction of the Judge's bench, seemingly unconcerned with what was about to happen.

Spending two nights in jail obviously had no effect on him. But Dale was always a hard guy to read, he rarely spoke up at family gatherings and acted as if he was only there in body and his mind was somewhere else. But Annie chose him to love and have children with. The family did their best to accept him, always trying to make him feel at home and part of the Gladstone clan.

The wrinkled suit at the other table had a stack of files piled in front of him. His pock-marked face buried in a folder held in his hands. He turned to the cop who nodded at JJ and started a conversation but the clerk stood up and called the courtroom to order. Maybe he was the new QRP detective in charge of the investigation.

He was clean-cut, if bald with a goatee fits that description. His suit wasn't as fancy as the one's worn by the Assistant Crown or Defense Lawyer. It resembled the one JJ was wearing, purchased on sale at Freeds. When he stood, he almost dropped the bunch of folders tucked under his arm. He appeared nervous. *Rookie detective*, JJ thought.

An older man with grey hair and John Lennon glasses, wearing a black robe, entered the courtroom from a door in the front wall and sat in the Judge's chair. Joseph Junior didn't think he looked like a Judge but really had no idea what one was supposed to look like. The robed man eyed the suited man with all the files on his desk and asked, "What have we got this morning?"

Unbeknownst to the Gladstone family and probably the majority of other people in the courtroom, the clerk controls the docket and decides which cases will be called first. When there are lawyers present, their cases are called up on a seniority basis. Richard Morris represented Dale Daniels. He had been practising law for over twenty years and his case was called first.

JJ heard her voice but couldn't tell you what the female court clerk looked like. His gaze was fixed on his ex-brother-in-law. He and his lawyer stood while she read the charge:

something about the first-degree murder of Annie Glad-stone/Daniels. If there was any noise in the room it had completely vanished when those three words rang out.

It was something you didn't hear every day, especially in a small town like Cooperville. According to police and citizens alike, Murder is considered the worst crime one person can commit upon another. One of the Ten Commandments: Thou Shalt Not Kill.

"Not Guilty." When asked for his plea, Dale answered like he was placing an order at a fast-food drive through. JJ felt heat in his neck and face, as if his blood was boiling. Not guilty? Really? Who seriously believed that? He turned to check on his father and brother. Jimmy clutched the top of the bench in front of him with both hands, his knuckles bloodless and white. Marie put her hand on JJ's thigh and started crying.

Not sure what was really going on, JJ listened while the assistant Crown and lawyer and Judge all talked about whether or not Dale should be released on bail. Released? Why would they arrest him, simply to release him? This wasn't a god-damned fishing derby. The man killed his sister. What the hell is going on? Is this how our justice system works?

The two legal eagles argued back and forth, the defense lawyer saying how Daniels was such a great guy and would be no danger to the public, should he be released. JJ stifled a laugh when they sparred over Dale's abstinence versus his known drinking and drug use. The Judge said he'd heard enough. Bail was denied. A uniformed police officer took control of Dale and they disappeared through another door in the wall.

Chapter Thirty Four

Satisfaction

There's a song by the Rolling Stones called '*Satisfaction*' (I can't get no). As the Gladstone family filed out of the courtroom, it was one word that ran through their minds. Dale was finally going to jail for killing Annie. How could any of them not be satisfied...at least a little. Sarah tried to handle questions from her children; what exactly did 'bail denied' mean? She was about to give it her best shot and answer the question when a detective from the QRP approached their group and identified himself.

Detective Walter Colley said he was assigned to the case as lead investigator after Martineau's retirement. He was the bald man with the black suit who sat in the front of the courtroom. He waited while the Gladstone's huddled in closer, before carrying on. Colley said Dale would be going to the county jail to await his trial, a date which would be some time in the future, depending on the court's calendar.

Sarah's youngest asked the question before anyone else could formulate one. "So, does that mean Uncle Dale killed Aunt Annie?"

The detective blushed at the question, obviously not prepared to explain the whole justice system to a grieving family with little to no experience in understanding the process. He went on to explain how Dale was 'arraigned' on the murder charge, where he publicly announced his innocence in front of a Justice. Then there was the matter of bail, which in his case, was denied.

Sarah noticed her father and Jimmy were absent from the group but she wanted to make sure she understood the process. Before she could ask, other family members chimed in with questions about jail and the future trial. JJ wanted to know why it took seven years to arrest Dale and what exactly prompted it.

The detective stuttered, trying to formulate an answer. Sarah noticed her big brother's face was red, again, and it looked as if his head was about to explode. He'd been the family spokesperson since the day Annie was struck down, and she often wondered if the ongoing stress would cause him to have a heart attack.

It was as if Colley was reading from a script when he said, "The investigation is ongoing and I can't give you any more details at this time." Sarah scoffed; a bit too loud. How many times had they heard that line? Did the police really know what they were doing? Why couldn't they simply tell them what exactly was going on? Was it a big secret?"

The detective's comment sent JJ and their mother off in another direction. Sarah had heard enough too. Or as much as they were ever going to hear, so it seemed. The rest of her clan broke apart like a football team leaving the huddle. Thinking they might want to do lunch somewhere downtown, Sarah tried to gather her immediate family outside the courthouse.

Jimmy paced back and forth on the sidewalk like an expectant father, waiting for the others. Sarah grabbed an arm on his way by and asked if he was okay. "What the fuck was that, sis, do the cops have any idea what they're doing?"

"I don't know, Jimmy, at least the bastard's going to jail."

Chapter Thirty Five

The County Gaol

The newest jail in the Windsor-Essex area is called the Southwest Detention Center. Formerly the County Gaol, its predecessor was so old its name was spelled in British English. Built in 1925, the old Windsor Jail showed its age inside and out. I'd visited there many times throughout my career, depositing and retrieving or meeting with inmates.

The aging jail, with stained cement walls topped by barbed wire, was like a rotting fortress in a historic west end neighborhood. To me, the hoosegow was more of a shithole inside the walls. Isn't that the way it's supposed to be? Except for staff, everyone inside was a criminal. Almost.

Many occupants were housed there while they awaited arraignments or trial dates, after being arrested. Those who were convicted of a crime and sentenced to two years, less a day, were kept in the county jail. Anyone sentenced to a deuce plus, was put into the federal system and incarcerated in places like Kingston Penitentiary.

The uneducated would assume that anyone spending time in jail received no special treatment and was served only bread and water. But those days are long gone. It might not be the best food in town, but inmates receive three squares a day, cooked in an onsite kitchen. There were no fast-food deliveries while inside, but I remember a staff strike when restaurant food was brought in.

When I was a child, my father served a thirty-day stint for assaulting a police officer during a labor strike he was involved in. He worked in the kitchen while incarcerated and told me he delivered a steak dinner to one inmate who threw the plate of food back at him. Convictions for assault police rarely consist of more than a monetary fine now days and perhaps it's a bit ironic that my father's son became a police officer.

In my humble opinion, prisoners are treated too well. They are criminals, after all, and jail is supposed to be punishment for crimes committed. Sure, there are rules and restrictions that would make life miserable for you and I if we spent time inside. But they are fed well and live rent free. I've come across criminals who consider jail time a badge of honor and mark themselves with ink to commemorate the event.

I've been told by some of my informants who spent time in jail, just how easy it is to get contraband and even illegal drugs. Spouses and sometimes lawyers, have been known to smuggle in illicit items. In one instance, I personally know of a man who got arrested just so he could deliver drugs to those inside. That usually meant swallowing or inserting foreign objects into their body cavities.

My informants also told me how some jail guards knew what was going on and looked the other way. On the flip side, one guard told me they were aware but sometimes ignored what was going on because it made prisoners more docile. I can't say I blame them. Just because a violent criminal is locked up, it doesn't mean he's not dangerous to jail staff or other inmates.

As a police officer, one of my favorite jobs was transporting prisoners to and from jail and to court. We called it the Chain Gang, where everyone was linked together by a long chain attached to their handcuffs. Sometimes leg restraints were included. Prisoners had to learn how to shuffle in sync as a group so as to not trip or fall. On more than one occasion, I witnessed seasoned convicts purposely trip up the new fish as an initiation.

There was always bitching and complaining when court ran late or inmates weren't returned to jail in time for their lunch or dinner. The menu at Windsor Police Headquarters was limited, they received a cheeseburger and juice box. In the old days, some cell keepers might accidentally microwave the burger a bit too long. The scalding hot cheese was a good remedy for loudmouths who thought they were staying at the Holiday Inn.

Chapter Thirty Six

Grieving

Sure, Dale Daniels was denied bail and sent to jail, but for how long? Jimmy Gladstone hoped he would rot in there but knew it wouldn't be the case. Ideas ran through Jimmy's head— maybe Dale would become someone's bitch inside and he'd learn something about pain or indignity. He could only wish.

It was his family's grieving through the whole ordeal that kept Jimmy down. He grew acutely aware of how his parents and siblings all handled Annie's death in different ways. Her murder completely ruined their family dynamic and became the main topic of conversation whenever they got together.

Jimmy knew he'd never forget but wanted to move on with his own life. He and his sister had been close but he knew Annie was gone forever. No more hanging out and listening to music together, like when they attended the Bluesfest on the Windsor waterfront. Music was only one of their connections, their children also hung out together.

Family gatherings got to the point of becoming painful, where Jimmy grew weary of everyone rehashing the fateful day and making themselves miserable. Their sadness only brought frustration and more tears. Even the children were torn, missing their aunt and embarrassed by their uncle.

Jimmy wondered how Dale could afford his high-priced lawyer since he didn't have that kind of money. JJ told him one of his friends paid Richard Morris a ten-thousand-dollar cash retainer to contest his impaired driving charge. And he'd heard about a guy at work who got busted for dealing cocaine, paying Morris a whopping thirty grand up front.

I had personally heard of such cash expenditures paid out to top-notch lawyers in an attempt to walk away from criminal charges. In many cases, having the money to pay for a great defense lawyer meant a better chance at an acquittal or at least a reduction in sentence. A prominent Windsor lawyer once bragged to me and some co-workers how he'd flash his gold Rolex to prospective clients, offering them a clue as to what his fees would be.

When the Gladstones learned that Dale's lawyer had taken on the case pro bono they were both shocked and angered. Why was he receiving such special treatment? Surely it wouldn't be the same for anyone else in their family if they were charged with a criminal offense. Jimmy asked a police detective what, exactly, did that mean.

The cop said Canadian law allows lawyers to take on pro bono cases where it's in the public's best interest, to preserve the rights of disadvantaged individuals. Jimmy almost blew a gasket when he heard the response and he laughed out loud. The officer admitted he completely understood. He said lawyers like Morris took on high-profile cases like Daniels' to gain attention and possible future business. It was advertising.

Jimmy asked himself how it could get any worse. Dale Daniels mentally abused his sister, killed her and then took her money and children. Now he'd hired one of the most expensive criminal lawyers in the province at no cost. What kind of world was he living in? Where was the thing they call justice? He thought about a saying he remembered, *'an eye for an eye, a life for a life'*. That was fair and just, as far as Jimmy Gladstone was concerned.

Chapter Thirty Seven

Pretrial Challenges

Definition of 'Trial' according to the Oxford Dictionary: *a formal examination of evidence before a Judge, and typically before a jury, in order to decide guilt in a case of criminal or civil proceedings.*

After Dale Daniels was arrested for the murder of his wife, Annie Gladstone Daniels, he was denied bail and sent to jail, awaiting his trial.

In Canada, the Crown Attorney may call for a Preliminary Inquiry to present the case to a Justice. During this inquiry the Crown produces witnesses to paint a picture of the alleged criminal offense. The goal being to convince the Judge that there is enough evidence to proceed to trial, before a higher court Judge and/or jury.

Defense Counsel is not required to present any evidence at this stage but can question witnesses to weigh their importance in the case or how it might affect the accused's guilt or innocence. It is an opportunity for the defense to evaluate the Crown's case against the accused.

In some instances, as in this case, there are pre-trial motions brought forward by defense counsel even before the preliminary inquiry begins. They receive full disclosure of the

Crown's case when charges are laid and then the defense picks their way through all the facts in evidence and witness statements to see what might be challenged constitutionally.

In the case against Dale Daniels, his lawyer challenged many of the search warrants executed by police, such as those obtained for his medical records. This can be very time consuming since a separate hearing must be held for each challenge, where information to obtain the warrant is picked apart line by line.

Even though the original warrant may have been signed by a Judge or Justice, the information supplied can be challenged by defense counsel. Investigators have to qualify their reasons for obtaining the warrant and satisfy the court that none of them infringed on the accused's civil rights in any way.

Morris challenged every warrant he could and although the court records of the pre-trial motions weren't made public, rumor was the Judge sided with defense counsel and tossed out many of the search warrants. This meant the Crown could not present any information or evidence that came as a result of those warrants. In layman's terms it's known as 'fruit of the poisonous tree'.

I attended many preliminary inquiries in my day, some with pre-trial motions. In those trials the whole process never lasted more than a day or two. In the case of Dale Daniels, the court set aside five weeks to hear witness testimony and the Crown's case.

Chapter Thirty Eight

Starting Lineup

Arriving at the court building on Monday morning, the first day of the scheduled preliminary inquiry for Dale Daniels, the Gladstone family was blown away by what they saw. People were lined up in freezing rain, waiting to clear security and enter the courthouse. Sarah Gladstone estimated there were about a hundred people in the queue.

Greetings were called out as they joined the line but faces were blurred, kind of like everything else that occurred over years passed. The endless stream of potential witnesses continued into the building and all the way to the courtroom. Sarah figured some of them had to be there as spectators. Surely, if there were that many witnesses, Dale would have been charged and convicted years earlier.

What appeared to the family as a circus event, was quietly discussed among Sarah, her siblings and parents. Once inside, more greetings and solemn nods came their way but the family kept to themselves, huddled in an alcove. Emotions ran high between them. Frustration, anger, grief, and even embarrassment. The Gladstone family had become a focal point for those lined up and crowded into the lobby outside the courtroom.

It was if everyone was staring at them but pretending not to. Sarah actually felt guilty, as if she and/or her family had done something wrong. All the attention over the years was stressful enough but this was almost humiliating. There was definitely something wrong with this picture. She could tell the others in her family were uncomfortable and felt the same way.

It got to the point where Sarah could feel the stares. Her gaze was drawn to one woman in particular. She remembered her eyes, such a dark shade of brown they looked black. It was as if an invisible laser beam shot across the room and burned an image onto Sarah's retina. It was the psychic. She couldn't remember her name.

The woman had been a previous employee at the family's corner store. Damn, what was her name? She showed up at the lunch counter one day after Annie's murder and spoke with Sarah's mother. Her father and brothers wanted nothing to do with the woman but Marie was willing to take any physical or spiritual help offered to her.

Marie let the woman use some of Annie's personal things and the psychic said she came to her, saying Dale did it—possibly with the help of one of his friends. She also mentioned two witnesses who were reluctant to come forward, one so upset they dropped out of school. The QRP interviewed the psychic but like everything else in their investigation, Sarah had no idea of the outcome.

Chapter Thirty Nine

Preliminary Inquiry

Along with one hundred or so potential witnesses and spectators, media were in attendance, interviewing anyone who'd allow a microphone or camera to be shoved in their face. The president of the local Criminal Lawyer's Association said he was surprised that so many witnesses had been called to testify at a preliminary hearing.

He said it was unusual, but personally didn't know anything about the case. Usually, the Crown will call sufficient evidence to secure a committal to trial but it varies from case to case. If Daniels was ordered to stand trial after the preliminary hearing, his case would be heard by a Judge and jury in Superior Court.

While the media and majority of the crowd milled about outside the courtroom, the case was called up, inside. An Ontario Court Justice presided. Two prosecutors sat a table below the bench. Two stacks of witness notices lay in front of Assistant Crown Attorneys Randal James and Rhonda Baker.

They called potential witnesses into the courtroom in small groups and told them what date to return for their testimony. They estimated between five and eight witnesses could testify each day, with another whole day set aside for one particular person. The Judge warned all witnesses they could face arrest if they failed to return to court when required.

As usual, there were scheduling conflicts between the Judge, prosecution and defense counsels, and available courtroom time. Even though the court docket had been previously cleared for an estimated five-week hearing, there were still going to be interruptions where they'd have to take breaks on certain days.

I had personally seen this type of controlled chaos on many occasions during my career, where defense lawyers normally held the case hostage because they'd scheduled themselves to be in two places at once. Like an overbooked hotel, it's peasants who suffer. In my experience the courts always bend over backwards, with Judges appeasing their fellow lawyers.

I had never heard of calling busloads of witnesses for a preliminary inquiry. Normally, the Crown only has to produce enough evidence to convince the court a crime has been committed. Was their case that week? Was their plan to bombard the justice with enough information he'd have to commit the case to trial?

If there was so much evidence and all those witnesses, why did the Queens Regional Police wait so many years to arrest and charge Dale Daniels? Was there a magic bullet or key piece of evidence that surfaced late in the game? If there was, investigators were tight-lipped and neither the media nor Gladstone family knew anything about it.

The noise in the hallway outside the courtroom was so loud, potential witnesses complained they couldn't hear their names being called over the public address system. It was a day of waiting for most; first standing outside in freezing temperatures, then the security line, and finally waiting in the hall for their names to be called.

Chapter Forty

Ducks in a Row

As with any type of criminal trial, potential witnesses are almost routinely asked to wait outside the courtroom until their names are called. They are also warned not to discuss the case with each other while waiting in the hall or lobby. This went for police investigators as well as civilian witnesses. They could talk about sports or the weather, but not their testimony or the case at hand.

As a rookie cop, waiting in the hallway for my turn to be called, a veteran detective once asked me to make sure two potential witnesses who were scheduled to testify were kept separate and not allowed to talk to each other outside the courtroom. I didn't take the simple request seriously and got my ass chewed out when the lead investigator saw the two witnesses having a chat nearby.

Personally, I've been questioned on the witness stand by defense counsel in open court as to whether or not I discussed the case with anyone outside the courtroom. They are afraid witnesses might compare notes or synchronize their testimony. The irony is defense lawyers often make deals or plea bargains in those same hallways.

In any preliminary inquiry or criminal trial, the Crown always has a plan or at least a preconceived idea of which witnesses to call first to prove their case in court. In theory they try to put their ducks in a row, producing witnesses to lay a roadmap the Judge and/or jury can follow to understand the crime that's been alleged to have been committed.

So, one at a time, Assistant Crown Randal James presented witnesses in the Dale Daniels case. Called first, were people who saw Annie run down by a hit and run driver so many years earlier. Like every other person on earth, their memories had faded with time. According to their testimony, they said they remembered the incident clearly; how a speeding red car hit Annie Gladstone and sent her flying through the air.

Those in the courtroom gallery displayed a variety of emotions as the hit and run was described in gruesome detail. Surprise, disbelief and even horror showed on solemn faces as first-hand witnesses recalled details from that tragic day. It was an event that obviously scarred some of them for life. All the witnesses said they were sure of what occurred; they were there and saw it happen, after all.

Richard Morris was an experienced defense lawyer with hundreds of criminal trials under his belt. He'd questioned thousands of witnesses and knew exactly how to approach each person just by looking at them. He hadn't become one of the province's best barristers solely by his seniority. His previous trial experience included the defense of some of Windsor's most notorious criminals.

It was all about reading and knowing people. What they reported to police or offered in their written statements was always open for interpretation. Police investigators and lawyers alike, have learned over the years that eye witnesses are never one hundred percent reliable. Memories fade but people also misread situations and make fatal mistakes 'thinking' they 'know' what they saw. A wise man once told me you can never believe anything you hear and only half of what you see. I have found it to be true.

There are several cases in Canada where people have been wrongfully arrested and convicted from eye witness testimony. Some of those spent decades in jail for criminal offenses they never committed. Others have been exonerated and released after new evidence was presented with things such as advances in DNA technology to prove their innocence.

Witnesses who previously testified were strategically attacked by Morris when cross examined. Although he tried, the skillful lawyer couldn't always achieve his goal of discrediting every witness with direct questions. One thing a good defense lawyer knows is that you never ask a question unless you already know the answer. If a defense counsel can prove a witness is biased or unreliable in any way, their testimony becomes irrelevant.

I'd fallen victim to Morris' tactics while being questioned by him on the witness stand. Defense counsel can't question a witness on facts that aren't already in evidence or previously presented by the Crown. They can make suggestions of scenarios, whether true or not, that might make a person second guess themselves. Many other lawyers use the same tactic but Richard Morris was a master at it.

He suggested that maybe the car was orange and not red. After testifying to the latter, one woman finally admitted she wasn't sure. Another believed a man was driving the car but later recanted, saying he couldn't describe the suspect and wasn't positive the driver was a man or woman. By the time Morris was done with the first few witnesses, it was unclear if the car was really red or even a car, and if the driver was a man or woman.

Differences in what speed the car was travelling also became an issue, whether or not the driver had time to avoid Annie Gladstone. Some witnesses thought the driver intentionally aimed the car at Annie and purposely tried to run her down. They'd reported to police the car was previously parked down the street, seemingly waiting for the victim to cross the road.

The skillful lawyer had one witness so twisted in thought, she wasn't sure if the car purposely hit Annie or she turned and unknowingly walked in front of it. It came down to should have, would have or could have. Witnesses who took the stand beaming with confidence, left confused and bewildered. Morris had them scratching their heads and wondering what they had really seen in the first place.

The next group of witnesses, Annie's boss and co-workers, didn't fare any better. Only witnessing the aftermath of the hit and run, they testified to previous events where Daniels showed up un-announced at the library to confront his estranged wife. They conveyed how afraid Annie was of Dale and how he seemed to be stalking her at the library and around town.

Defense counsel dismissed them and their testimony with a few simple questions—basically getting them to admit they had no proof it was Dale who ran his wife down, and how him 'confronting' her could be easily explained by Dale simply wanting to talk to his wife about their children.

One by one, Richard Morris took witnesses who appeared to be completely reliable and poked holes in their testimony. It's probably the reason the Crown decided not to call any of the children who witnessed the hit and run. Grown teenagers at the time, they were barely old enough to understand what they'd seen as children, let alone recall and testify to what they saw so many years earlier.

There had been plenty of discussion among police investigators immediately after the incident, when the school children were questioned as to what they witnessed. There were too many differences in details and descriptions, specifics that would only hurt the case down the road when it got to court. Assistant Crown Randal James was aware of that fact and knew better than to present more unreliable witnesses.

For those seated in the court gallery seeing the trial unfold, it was like watching the final game in major league baseball's world series. The Crown sent up their best hitters to the plate early in the lineup, only to have them struck out by the opposing pitcher. No hits meant no one on base and no runs scored. No runs meant there was no chance of winning. It was time to change the line up.

Chapter Forty One

Designated Hitters

Hoping to at least score a run and try to convince the Judge that they really could win the game, Assistant Crown Randall James called up a pinch hitter. Since the string of eye witnesses called to the stand so far had only blurred the image of what actually transpired during the collision between an automobile and Annie Gladstone, the prosecutor brought in an expert witness.

Normally reserved for jury trials, a Queen's Regional Police Accident Re-constructionist was called to the stand to give expert testimony. These officers receive special training above and beyond what regular patrol officers get. They learn calculations and specifics, taught by traffic engineers and planners, on how to investigate and physically recreate the scene of a collision.

Measurements, photographs and numeric formulas are used to pinpoint the exact location of impact, taking into consideration fixed points of reference to estimate things like the speed of an automobile prior to the collision. Once an accident reconstructionist is qualified as an expert witness in court, they can offer opinion evidence as to what they believe occurred at the time of the event.

Having been previously declared an expert witness in certain narcotics several times during my career, I understand the process more than the lay person. Whether a previously accepted expert witness or not, police and other professionals first have to prove or qualify their expertise to the court. If accepted, only then can they give testimony in the form of opinion evidence. So, each time an expert wants to testify as such, they must first prove their expertise to the court.

It sounds ridiculous, but potential experts have to keep an up-to-date C.V. (curriculum vitae) that spells out any experience that might qualify them as an expert. In my case it was my narcotics training, number of arrests, drug seizures, and interviews with users and dealers where I learned about certain drug subcultures that led to my expertise. It's the same with an accident re-constructionist but with a whole different set of qualifications.

Once the potential expert takes the witness stand, the prosecution poses questions to expose qualifications and any expertise in their particular field. The defense can either accept the qualifications as presented or question the potential expert to determine the validity of facts presented. If unchallenged by defense counsel the Judge has the final say in declaring the witness as an expert.

Normally, opinion evidence is not allowed by any witness giving testimony—only things personally observed can be attested to. It is only when a Judge declares a witness an expert, they are allowed to offer opinion evidence.

The re-constructionist brought visual aids to the witness stand and displayed a scaled diagram, depicting the scene of the collision. According to him, he took things like tire marks and debris on the road into account, as well as damage to the suspect vehicle. Finally, he considered Annie's injuries and the eventual resting position of her body after being struck.

Using his personal measurements and calculated formulas, the specialist estimated the location and speed of the vehicle just prior to and at the exact time of impact. He estimated the red Camaro was traveling at 75 kilometers per hour, 35 kph over the posted speed limit, when it struck Annie Gladstone.

Richard Morris listened to the police expert and spent a moment taking in the detailed diagram before his cross-examination. He simply asked the officer if he had any way of knowing exactly who was driving the vehicle in question at the time of the collision. Expecting to be questioned on things like mathematical calculations or formulas, the officer had to agree with defense counsel that he had no idea who was operating the vehicle.

Hoping family members might help to bolster his languishing case, the Crown called the Gladstones to testify next. Joe Junior had come to court prepared. He'd kept personal notes from the time Annie and Dale began having marital problems. His entries were hand-written, noting dates and times he'd seen or heard his ex-brother-in-law flirting with a co-worker and cheating on his sister.

Police investigators were aware of his written chronology and he'd supplied them with statements on more than one occasion to that effect. Having never been to court, JJ was nervous on the witness stand. He stood proud, waiting to defend his sister's honor and seek justice.

He eyed Dale from his perch on the witness stand. His ex-brother-in-law had either lost weight or couldn't find proper clothes to fit him. JJ didn't care either way. He'd once accepted him as family but never really liked him as much as everyone else. There was something about him. Dale wore the same dazed and blank look JJ had seen so many times in the past at family gatherings. It was as if the man really wasn't there.

Prepared for an onslaught of questions to answer years of reported information to the police, JJ was taken aback by defense counsel's questions about Dale's truck. Richard Morris seemed particularly interested in the doors—how many there were and which way they opened. The eldest Gladstone son was completely thrown for a loop. What the hell did truck doors have to do with anything?

Jimmy Gladstone felt like someone kicked him in the groin when his name was called. The long walk to the witness stand was like running the gauntlet at the end of a marathon. He felt everyone's stare and nobody was cheering him on. Jimmy was elated to finally see an end to his lifelong nightmare in sight, but he was concerned about tripping and falling flat on his face. Faces on either side of the isle were blurred and distorted, like in a painting by Matisse.

Taking the witness stand and turning to face the court, Dale's was the first face Jimmy saw. He had a clear view of the devil himself. His sister's killer showed no sign of remorse. Jimmy couldn't believe it was the same man he used to drink beer and jam with. They both played guitar and shared a love of rock and roll music. There had been a time when they both shared a love for Annie.

Those memories were now stored in a weathered old cardboard box in the back of Jimmy's brain. A single thought burned through his frontal cortex. The impulse to lunge from the witness stand and strangle the shit out of Dale. He wondered if he could get away with it. Could it be called justifiable homicide? Could he claim temporary insanity? Most would agree it was justified; he thought.

Richard Morris asked him point blank if he thought Dale Daniels killed his sister. The whole process—the hit and run, hospital, funeral, police investigation, and being asked to rehash the details over and over had been a horrible thing to go through. In answer to the lawyer's question, Jimmy can't be sure if he only thought the response or actually said it out loud. He believes it was something like, 'You're fucking right I do'.

Sarah followed her brothers, shaking like a leaf in the wind when she took the witness stand. She had hoped not to have to look at Dale but he was hard to miss, sitting beside his lawyer at the front of the courtroom. Facing the gallery, Sarah wanted to take in other faces in the room, but her eyes wouldn't stray from the evil man her sister once loved.

Dale didn't make eye contact with Sarah. She wanted to call out, 'Hey, look at me you bastard'. He was a coward as far as she was concerned; the things he said and did to Annie. A spineless man who fooled the whole family and especially her sister. She wondered why he cut his hair so short after the murder. Did he change his appearance on purpose? There were so many things she wanted to say to him.

The Assistant Crown interrupted her train of thought. Years of elapsed time dulled Sarah's memory of what she testified to that day. Questions from Randall James were like hearing a scratchy old tape recording that had been played over and over again. Although she wasn't there when Annie was run down, Sarah felt guilty and had always wondered if there was anything else she could have done to prevent it.

She testified to her sister's marital discord and the many teary conversations she'd had with Annie while she was trying to deal with Dale during their separation. She tried to talk about the abuse and stalking, most of which was objected to by defense counsel as hearsay. What did he mean? Why couldn't she testify to what they talked about? It was all very confusing.

Matters only got worse when Sarah was questioned by Richard Morris. He didn't want to hear anything bad that she'd testified to about Dale. The fork-tongued lawyer steered her in a direction she wasn't prepared for, trying to get Sarah to admit how good of a father Dale was. Morris suggested the only reason Daniels stalked Annie was to talk about the children and try to put their marriage back together.

Suggestions about how great a guy Dale was made Sarah furious. She was frustrated that she wasn't allowed to emphasize just how afraid Annie was of him. The surprise appearances at her home, work, and even in traffic on the street. When Morris suggested that it had been too many years and perhaps her memory had faded, Sarah almost lost it. She mentally blocked out anything about the trial after that.

Chapter Forty Two

Life Goes On

Being retired from the police service and out of the loop, I had no idea what was going on with the Dale Daniels preliminary hearing for his murder charge. At some point I'd stopped reading the Windsor Star and I never watched or listened to news broadcasts of any type. I'd seen enough depressing crap as a cop, stuff that normally made up the daily news. When curious, I kept up with world events digitally. The Internet was my source of information.

A post on one of my social media pages caught my eye. It was an article about the Daniels trial, saying over a hundred witnesses would be called to testify. Having never heard of such ridiculous numbers at a preliminary inquiry, I was blown away. After that sunk in, I thought about the Gladstone family. I hadn't seen any of them in a while and couldn't even imagine the turmoil they were going through.

Curiosity got the best of me and I clicked on links attached to the article. I hated how reporters and news agencies always re-hashed all the details of an event, in case someone reading it was just tuning in. Where was the sympathy for victims? Families like the Gladstones had to relive Annie's death over and over and over, again and again.

I thought about myself for a moment, the drama and turmoil I'd lived through the previous few years. My separation and divorce, the move back to the city, and my own loss of loved ones. Getting back into the dating game was a whole new adventure in itself. But visiting my mother and father in the hospital at the same time was a sad experience that motivated me to get on with my own life.

Cancer eventually claimed my mother but my father recovered from his heart attack. Considering my grief, I wondered if I was abnormal or something was wrong with me. I never cried at funerals and even my best friend questioned me about it on one occasion. I had to identify a close friend's body as it lay in a ditch after he took his own life. My tears were only shed when I saw one of his young son's carrying his police hat at the funeral.

But why didn't I cry when my own mother died, and later when my father also passed. I remembered shedding plenty of tears when my marriage fell apart. For some reason, death didn't affect me in the same way. I'd seen plenty of it during my career in policing. Everyone else I knew seemed to automatically turn on the waterworks when someone close to them passed.

For me, death is a natural part of life. Something that's beyond our control, so to speak. It's been said that we start dying the day we are born. It's true. Some people can't handle hearing that and refuse to talk about the end of the road. Not me. I've always lived life large and death doesn't really scare me. Not that I wish to leave this earth ahead of schedule but when my time comes, I'd like to think I'll be okay with it.

Obviously, I handle grief differently than most people. Everyone reacts in their own way, a fact that I've witnessed personally over time. I clicked on another article about Annie Gladstone's murder and wondered why the hell it took the cops so long to arrest her killer and get him into court? When it came to their grief, I could only imagine how the Gladstone family felt.

Chapter Forty Three

Dazed and Confused

Physically and mentally struggling through the exhaustive preliminary hearing was another marathon the Gladstone's had to endure. It's not like they had any choice. Seeing Annie's killer brought to justice had become an unintended mission in their lives. Going to court was like living in the movie *Ground Hog Day*. They existed in a fog that never seemed to clear.

It was stress to the 10th degree. They all had lives beyond the courthouse, never could they have imagined having to basically live there. Waiting all those years for Daniels to be arrested was bad enough, but having to hear and talk about him every day was not only frustrating but extremely depressing. He wasn't only in their family discussions but with everyone else who hung around the courthouse.

Collectively, they joked if they had a dollar for every time someone asked one of them how they were, they could afford an all-inclusive family vacation. It's not that they didn't appreciate the concern and well-wishers who sought them out daily. It was just tiring. So tiring and time-consuming, they had to hire extra help to run the family business.

Jimmy and his father used work as an excuse to slip away from the trial when they'd had enough but Marie refused to leave, feeling she'd be abandoning her daughter. Whether it would be good or bad for them individually or as a family, a bone of contention was they weren't allowed to remain in the courtroom until they testified.

Spectators who had nothing to do with the case knew more about what was happening than they did. And the police couldn't be bothered to give them a play-by-play action report or keep them abreast of how the case was going. Not only did they live in a constant fog, the family was kept in the dark, like mushrooms.

Adding to the Gladstones' pain was the fact Annie's children didn't want to talk to them. Or at least that's what they were told. Someone said Dale let them read all the police reports, hearing what the family had to say about him, how they made him out to be the bad guy. Christopher and Ashley were mentally pulled in two separate directions ever since their mother was run down. They would never know if their father was their mother's killer.

Annie Gladstone's family went above and beyond what most normal people had to endure after the death of a loved one. They attended the trial faithfully, watching extended family and friends, and even strangers wearing out hinges on the courtroom door as they entered and exited after testifying. The Gladstone's found no hope in dejected and solemn faces of witnesses as they left the courtroom.

Chapter Forty Four

Police Witnesses

The dozens of civilian witnesses called to the stand during the preliminary inquiry were picked apart one by one by Richard Morris. If he wasn't working pro-Bono, one would have to say he was earning his money. After hearing a similar story from everyone who testified, the sitting Justice and anyone else with half a brain could easily come to the conclusion Annie Gladstone was killed by a hit and run driver.

With all the testimony heard so far, it was only conjecture that the driver of the car intentionally struck Annie. There was no physical proof of that theory. To Randal James and the Gladstone family's frustration, it had not been proven Dale Daniels was driving the vehicle that killed his wife.

In preliminary inquiries I'd been involved in, the Crown's first witness was usually someone who'd actually seen the crime committed. Failing that, they called the responding police officer(s) first on scene. Either witness can be used as a starting point to show the lay of the land and describe the alleged crime.

It's almost funny. I say *alleged* because I've caught many criminals red-handed or in the act of committing a crime, but it still has to be proven beyond a reasonable doubt in a court of law, before their guilt may be proclaimed. In the Daniels case, the Crown opted to produce witnesses from the scene of the crime to lay the foundation of their case.

The first responders weren't called until later because the initial involvement was mainly to control the chaos on their arrival. They weren't in any position to start taking measurements, thus the collision reconstructionist became a more essential witness. His expert testimony and accompanying detailed diagrams accurately describing the scene of the collision kept the court focussed on the sequence of events.

Calling officers first on scene last, really didn't help the Crown's case. They didn't tell the court anything it hadn't already heard in regard to the location of the collision or what eye-witnesses reported. But James seemed bent on playing on the Judge's emotions as he droned on and on about Annie's serious injuries and the traumatized children who witnessed the event.

Richard Morris made quick work of the first responders as well as other police officers who attended the scene and dealt with witnesses. Basically, he shot down their testimony by asking them if they or any of the people they interviewed could identify Dale Daniels as the person who was driving the hit and run vehicle.

It was the same with officers who recovered the red Camaro and spoke to its owner after he reported his car stolen. Daniels' defense was obvious, being played over and over as witness after witness admitted that they couldn't put him behind the wheel of the car that struck Annie Gladstone. There was no proof he was at the scene of the crime at the time of the occurrence.

The Crown produced paramedics and even doctors who testified to Annie's fatal injuries but once again, their testimony did nothing to prove that her estranged husband had anything to do with causing the injuries that led to her death.

Chapter Forty Five

The Professionals

I have been involved in preliminary inquiries where the presiding Judge stopped the proceedings part-way through and announced that he/she was satisfied there was enough evidence presented by the Crown to commit the case to trial. Even though the Daniels inquiry had dragged on for weeks with dozens of witnesses testifying, this didn't happen.

Assistant Crown Attorney Randall James trudged on, calling various Queen's Regional Police Detectives to the stand. A few years into retirement, Antoine Martineau was eventually called to testify. He explained how his investigation picked up where first responding officers left off. Other detectives attended the scene of the crime and re-interviewed witnesses.

Detective Martineau painted a grim picture of how the victim appeared to him when he saw her in the hospital. The veteran police officer had seen all kinds of injured, mutilated, and dead bodies during his career but when asked to describe Annie Gladstone's condition, his eyes watered and there was a hitch in his voice.

The QRP detective walked the court through Annie's ordeal, how she was injured so badly she had to be taken to Detroit for expert medical care. Martineau had followed along, giving the family some distance while they tried to wrap their heads around what had transpired. All the while, police investigators gathered information that left them with serious questions about the possibility of Annie's estranged husband's involvement.

The veteran detective said witnesses provided statements about Daniels' behaviour before the incident, and how he was stalking Annie while they were separated and living apart. Email and phone records confirmed that information. Martineau also mentioned that trace evidence—carpet fibres found in the stolen vehicle were similar to those found in Daniels' home.

The detective said it was he and his partner who visited the suspect and notified him of his wife's passing. Martineau admitted he'd made dozens of similar notifications over the thirty-year span of his career but he was taken aback by Daniels' reaction. What he could only describe as an over-the-top theatrical display of emotion.

The seasoned investigator was fully aware that everybody grieves and accepts loss in their own way but Daniels put on quite a show. Odd, Martineau thought, since everyone he interviewed or spoke to said how quiet, reserved and laid-back the man was. Defense counsel objected, citing the hearsay rule applied to what others told the detective. It was one of only a few objections Morris made during the detective's testimony. Instead, he busied himself scribbling on a notepad, no doubt waiting for his cross-examination.

Randal James coaxed detective Martineau on, getting what he considered important follow-up investigation onto the record. Discarded DNA, surveillance, search warrants, and wiretap evidence was presented. Morris interjected and reminded the detective he couldn't testify in regard to the warrants that were excluded in the pre-trial.

Other Q.R.P. detectives followed Martineau, sharing details of their involvement in the lengthy murder investigation. The parade of police witnesses quickly turned into a repeat performance of the civilians that preceded them. Everything they testified to and put into evidence by the Crown was quickly rebutted by Richard Morris.

Daniels' defense had become so obvious it could have been displayed on a billboard on the courtroom wall above the Justice's head. There was no need for the hot-shot lawyer to spell it out. None of the Crown witnesses provided a shred of proof that Dale Daniels was in any way involved in the actual death of Annie Gladstone.

Chapter Forty Six

Sundays

Marie Gladstone loved Sundays. To her, it was family day. Granted, they still had a business to run but they only served breakfast and lunch throughout the week. Sunday afternoons were busy with the after-church crowd, but dinner time was all about family. There was no excuse for non-attendance, anyone doing so would face the wrath of mom. Even regular customers knew better than to visit the store during Sunday dinner time.

Jimmy thought it more important to stay and play baseball with his buddies one Sunday. Trying to use an excuse of extra innings did nothing to get him out of dish duty for the next whole week. Even after complaining a flat tire caused him to be late for dinner on another occasion, Joe Junior had to produce the damaged rubber before his mother excused him.

The matriarch of the Gladstone clan accepted how her children had all grown up and started their own families, but the once-a-week sit down dinner was her way of instilling a sense of community. It was a tradition her parents passed on to her. The Sunday dinner table was the place to share their lives with each other and be thankful for what God had given them.

Marie went all out for the weekly feast. That usually meant a huge turkey, honey-baked ham or some type of pot roast. Any leftovers were put into sandwiches and soups, sold at the lunch counter. Regular customers knew Mondays were best to score things like a clubhouse with real turkey or homemade pea soup with bite-sized chunks of ham.

But since Annie's death, Sundays had become more of a chore for Marie, not knowing what to prepare for dinner or even having the energy to make it. Dale's trial became ridiculously taxing on all of them so she completely understood when one of her other children asked to be excused. It had gotten so bad that Marie committed a mortal sin one Sunday—ordering pizza instead of cooking.

Joseph Gladstone saw what had become of his remaining family after Annie's death and he was not happy. Even for those who knew him well, it was hard to decipher his demeanor and true feelings. He'd always thought of his wife as the matriarch who held his family together but since the loss of his youngest daughter, he wondered if he was wrong.

Annie was such a bright and cheerful person who made everyone feel better about themselves, just by being around her. She possessed an unearthly aura that seemed to encompass anyone who was near her. Sure, Joe loved all his other children just as much, but Annie was special and easily daddy's little girl. Losing her took his breath away, as if someone ripped out one of his lungs.

Since the trial, Sundays had become a day to escape from reality. Joe tried to busy himself on Saturdays, working around the garage, but the mind is a difficult thing to turn off. And Sunday dinners just weren't the same. The solemn faces around the dinner table and lack of lively conversation were only reminders of the grief on everyone's mind.

Marie ordering pizza for family dinner was a kick in the gut for Joe. Until that point, he'd thought his wife had a handle on things. He fooled no one, everyone knew it was Marie who was the real head of the family. Joe accepted that, knowing he simply lacked the emotional capacity to be there for them like she could.

Sarah Gladstone loved their Sunday family dinners. It was a tradition her children seemed to enjoy and she hoped they would carry on when they had their own offspring. But for her, Sundays weren't the same without her sister, Annie. Sometimes life got in the way and the week flew by without them finding time to talk. Sunday dinner was their chance to catch up. Who else could she talk to about the kids or their husbands?

Since Annie's death, family dinners became depressing. She knew everyone was grieving, how could they not. She may have been the youngest but Annie seemed to have a special bond with each one of them in a different way. A certain knack for knowing exactly how to connect with people, perhaps. Everyone thought their mother was the glue that held the family together but in truth, it was Annie.

Of course, Sarah loved her parents and even her brothers. Many times, while they were growing up, it was the boys against the girls but she secretly loved the rivalry. Annie may have been much younger but she was always there to back up her big sister. That kind of age gap could have easily enlarged as they grew older but it only brought them closer.

Sunday dinners almost became unbearable for Jimmy Gladstone. The trial weighed heavy on everyone's mind but he hated how it had become the focus of family conversations. Frustrated and worn out by hanging around the courtroom all week, Jimmy usually looked forward to their Sunday get-togethers. He knew how upset everyone else was over Annie's death and the bullshit trial they had to endure each day. Why did they have to re-hash everything at Sunday dinner?

Jimmy grew angrier with each day of the preliminary inquiry. He couldn't understand the lengths the Crown Attorney was going through to prove Dale's guilt. Everyone knew he killed Annie. Did they not have enough proof to send the asshole back to jail? He'd heard jokes about how slowly the wheels of justice turned but this was ridiculous.

There was one thing that haunted Jimmy when he was trying to fall asleep at night. What would happen if Dale beats this thing? Was that possible? They'd heard nothing positive from the police, and the Crown had not spoken to them since they were individually called to the witness stand. Left in the dark, as they had been through most of this ordeal, Jimmy could only cross his fingers and toes and hope for the best.

Sunday dinner was all about the food for JJ Gladstone. He loved his mother's cooking, especially her pork roast with roasted potatoes, carrots and onions. There were always leftovers so he'd sneak himself a doggie bag to take home, before mom packed it up to make soup and sandwiches. JJ liked to chop up the potatoes and onions to make himself corned beef hash.

Being the eldest and biggest sibling, he always managed to get more than his share at the dinner table. The downside was it had grown on him, literally. JJ had become acutely aware the rest of his family counted on him to keep them updated about the police investigation into Annie's death and even Dale's trial. Not sure he was happy about being the family spokesperson, JJ figured it was the least he could do for them.

And he had done pretty well at keeping everyone informed throughout the whole ordeal, until the powers stopped informing him. It started when Detective Martineau retired. It was as if he had formed a bond with the family. He really showed he cared. Information from the police became scarce after that, like the Gladstone family didn't matter anymore.

Many of JJ's calls to investigators went unanswered, and when they were he was simply told the investigation was ongoing. If he had a dollar for every time he heard that phrase, JJ figured he'd be a rich man. It was the same during the preliminary inquiry, trying to get any information or updates from the police or Crown was like pushing a car uphill. Usually in the know, JJ felt he was letting his family down.

The trial had dragged on for weeks and still Joseph Junior had no idea if Dale was ever going to be found guilty of killing his little sister. Another Sunday came around and JJ looked forward to one of his mother's home-cooked meals. He knew it would be turkey since mom asked his wife if she could bring her special cranberry sauce.

When the phone rang, JJ assumed it was Jimmy, they liked to bet on what mom would be cooking that day. The bet was a lock with his inside knowledge. He was disappointed when he didn't recognize the voice, the caller was female and identified herself as Rhonda Baker, the Assistant Crown Attorney. JJ had never spoken to her but recognized the name. She asked if he could round up the rest of the family and meet her and Randall James downtown.

Chapter Forty Seven

The Meeting

JJ felt a tightening sensation in his stomach and it wasn't hungering pangs in anticipation of Sunday dinner. Of course, the Assistant Crown didn't elaborate, only requesting a meeting with the family before they all returned to court on Monday. Not sure exactly why, he called Jimmy first. His brother responded, 'It's about time that fucker goes down'. JJ presumed Jimmy was referring to Dale making some kind of a deal by pleading guilty, something they'd heard might be a possibility way back when.

Excited and sounding more positive than he had been in years, the younger brother said he'd call their folks. JJ agreed and said he'd get in touch with Sarah and they could all meet at his place to take the van downtown. Her eldest brother blurted out the news before Sarah could say hello. She asked if there was anyone else who she should call, and agreed to meet at JJ's place.

In less than an hour, the Gladstone family was gathered at JJ's house. Conversation was more upbeat than usual, with them kibitzing and guessing as to what kind of a deal Dale had taken. Phrases like, 'It's about time that bastard gets what he's got coming' and 'I hope he rots in jail' were thrown around and discussed. Marie only cried and never said a word. Joseph almost cracked a smile, hoping his family's ordeal was about to come to an end.

Maybe it was the lack of Sunday traffic or because everyone's minds were racing with thoughts of closure, JJ seemed to make the drive to the Crown Attorney's office in record time. Finding a parking spot wasn't a problem either, they'd been paying dearly at metered lots every day of the trial. The court building was deserted, something else they had never witnessed.

Assistant Crown Attorney's Randal James and Rhonda Baker could have been in a Texas hold'em poker tournament, wearing expressionless faces when they greeted the Gladstone's. None of them dared ask why they were there. They quietly took their places in chairs laid out for them. James thanked them all for coming, saying he wanted to personally keep them abreast of what was going on with the trial. Jimmy scoffed a bit too loud at the comment.

The Assistant Crown Attorney went into a long-winded spiel about how difficult the case had been to prosecute, with a lack of direct evidence and their inability to disprove the alibi Daniels provided to police. He dropped a bomb which made no noise whatsoever. He said they were withdrawing the murder charge against Dale Daniels.

His words hung in the air like an autumn fog. Scoffs and gasps fell from open mouths on stunned faces. Shock and dismay are only two of the emotions that quickly filled the hearts and souls of the Gladstone family. Heads turned, checking each other to see if everyone else had just heard the same thing. Withdraw the murder charge? What, exactly, did that mean?

Randal James went into another spiel how the Crown failed to prove their case thus far and even if they proceeded with the preliminary inquiry, there was no reasonable prospect of a conviction on the murder charge. Before anyone could ask, James nodded solemnly and said, 'The charge will be withdrawn tomorrow and accordingly, Dale Daniels will be released from custody'.

Chapter Forty Eight

Aftermath

The ride home from the courthouse was painfully quiet. The kind of quiet you might find standing in an abandoned graveyard. Quiet that was eventually interrupted by sobbing and sniffles. The normally faint sound of rubber tires on pavement roared like a jumbo jet taking off. The minivan's little squeaks and rattles echoed in Jimmy's ears. He welcomed the distractions. He hated silence.

Jimmy asked his brother to turn the radio on. Music was his escape and he hoped it might help sooth the rest of his family's pain...fat chance...there was no cure for that kind of pain. He looked at his parents and siblings, one by one. How could they ever recover from this? It was bad enough losing Annie. Now Dale would go free? How would they live with that? There was no justice. Jimmy listened to the music and tried to lose himself in the sound of an acoustic guitar.

Everyone quietly went their separate ways after arriving at JJ's house. Jimmy and his wife went straight home. He caught Mary staring at him a few times but refrained from making eye contact for fear of breaking down and driving off the road. When he got home, Jimmy felt like he'd just run a marathon. His shoes felt as if they weighed fifty pounds each but his load didn't lighten when he kicked them off at the door.

The kids were home but he couldn't face them. He'd let Mary deal with it, she was better at that kind of thing. Jimmy couldn't remember grabbing a beer from the fridge but found one in his hand when he put his feet up and collapsed into his favorite recliner. He didn't remember turning the stereo on either. Weird. Exhaustion clouded his thoughts. The years, months, weeks and days since Annie's death had taken their toll. Jimmy nodded off.

When he woke there was an empty beer bottle in his hand and three more on the end table beside him. Jimmy had no recollection of drinking them but he wanted more. He needed to forget. Or did he need to remember? Annie invaded his thoughts so often. He wasn't sure how he got to the Canada Tavern and had forgotten they changed the name. It looked the same inside. Jimmy was pleasantly surprised to see JJ there, someone to drown his sorrow with.

They sat at a corner table in silence, nursing their beers. Sarah came in and joined them. His brother must have called her since it wasn't a place she normally hung out. Jimmy recognized a song from Journey on the jute box, one that he and Annie heard the band play live at Pine Knob. A young woman walked in the front door, swaying to the music and lip-syncing the words to the song. From a distance, he thought it was Annie.

But it wasn't her. Dale Daniels was right behind the woman. He bobbed his head to the music, like he used to do when he and Jimmy jammed together. Unbelievable. He was out of jail already, free as a bird, with a woman who could have been Annie's twin. He wore a smile worthy of a man who just beat a murder rap. What an asshole.

Jimmy turned to his brother and sister to gauge their reactions but they were gone. He sat alone. The sound of breaking glass came from behind the bar. Jimmy thought he recognized a man talking to the bartender. He looked like that cop, Norm Strom. Fucking police. Why couldn't they do their job and put Dale in jail for life. Jimmy heard a sharp crack and turned to the pool table.

His ex-brother-in-law was shooting pool. The woman he came in with was gone. JJ stood at the opposite end of the table, pool cue in hand. Dale was a shitty pool player but he made an impossible shot, then glanced up at Jimmy and smiled. What the hell was going on...why was JJ shooting pool with that bastard? Jimmy squeezed his beer glass so hard that it shattered in his hand. Staring at the cut in his palm, he made a fist and watched blood drip down his arm.

He held his bloody fist in the air and charged toward the pool table. Dale didn't see him coming, he was kissing the woman. She was back. Just as Jimmy got within striking distance, Dale threw Annie's lookalike to the floor. She lay there looking broken, bleeding from a severe head wound. It was his sister. Jimmy went berserk. Someone grabbed his shoulder to hold him back.

When he opened his eyes, Mary was standing over him. His fist was still clenched and he checked his palm for blood. There was no injury. Jimmy was confused. He was still in his recliner, Mary at his side, rubbing his shoulder. Trying to clear the fog from his brain, he stumbled for words and told his wife he must have dozed off. She nodded and said, 'You must have had a bad dream...you were screaming at Dale".

Chapter Forty Nine

LIfe With Dad and Without Mom

Christopher and Ashley were very young when their mother was struck down by a hit and run driver. Young enough they weren't really sure what it meant when they found out her death was being investigated as a murder. It was bad enough other kids in the neighborhood and at school stared at them after Annie Gladstone's highly publicized death. When rumors spread that their own father might somehow be responsible, their lives changed forever.

Ashley was like her mom, likable and outgoing, someone who easily made friends and had lots of them. Realization that her confidant and best female friend was gone forever, the normally cheerful young girl chose isolation. She withdrew from her circle of friends and dropped out of Girl Guides and the school drama club. Ashley couldn't understand why she was cut off from seeing her grandparents and cousins and didn't believe what her father said about them.

She also hated the fact her dad had a girlfriend. Ashley had heard him on the phone telling her mom how much he loved her and wanted to be a family again. If that was true, why was he with another woman? Her mother used to answer questions like that. But after her death there was no one else she could turn to. Her brother wasn't any help, he said there was no way their father had anything to do with their mother's death.

Christopher was confused. He chose a different path in life than his sister but shied away from his friends too. It seemed they all had questions or made inappropriate comments about something personal that was none of their business. Christopher was smart enough to know what was printed in the newspaper wasn't always true. He spent hours surfing the internet, doing his own investigating in search of the truth.

His father could be distant and even an asshole at times, but Christopher honestly didn't believe him capable of killing his mother. He had his suspicions years later, when his dad was arrested for murder. He and Ashley were both shocked when he was taken into custody. The police wouldn't have arrested him if they didn't think he killed their mother. Would they? What was already a screwed-up life for the Daniels children, became their living nightmare.

Christopher devoured any newspaper articles he could find and watched television news day and night searching for updates. Did his father really do it? Could he? Everyone seemed to think so. They kept his dad in custody and he wasn't allowed to see him. Maybe if he could talk to his father maybe he would say what was really going on. Surely, he would tell his own son if he killed their mother. If it was true, the young man needed to understand why.

Although unplanned and unexpected, Christopher and Ashley eventually got to see their grandparents and extended family. With their father in jail, Children's Aid first seized custody of them. Guardianship didn't come easy for the elder Gladstones and they had to take the matter to court. Thankfully, common sense won the day and the siblings were given back to their natural family.

Being with grandparents who loved her, wasn't enough to save Ashley from her emotional slide into a depressed state. After years of questions and accusations about her mother and father, she was no longer the happy-go-lucky girl she once was. Ashley lost interest in helping out with the family business and spent most days secluded in her room, crying or reading romance novels with happy endings.

Christopher didn't fare any better with the change in venue. He started acting out, cutting classes at school and sneaking out of the house at night. His grandparents retired early in the evening, giving him time to prowl at night and get into trouble with new friends of the same mind. After the police brought him home one night, the elder Gladstones felt it was time for another change.

Uncle Jimmy and Aunt Mary took Christopher in, hoping the close relationship with his cousins might help to settle him back into some type of normal life. But he didn't change and stayed up into the night, spending hours on the internet in chat rooms with other misfits who put all kinds of ideas in his head. He ignored his cousin's friendship and soon rebelled against any type of authority, including his aunt and uncle.

The years while their father spent in custody waiting for his trial didn't help matters for either child. They were no longer children. They had questions. It had gotten to the point where everyone believed their father murdered their mother. Christopher and Ashley never wanted to believe it was true but they had to live with everyone else's belief. How could they ever come to grips with that?

Their father's trial wreaked even more havoc on their already tormented minds and souls. It dragged on and on. They weren't alone, even their grandparents and aunts and uncles were emotional wrecks. Their family's tragedy made headlines in the media once again. To make matters worse, Christopher and Ashley had no idea what was happening in court. Making only brief appearances to testify, was the only time they were allowed in the courtroom.

It drove Christopher nuts; the publications ban during the trial left him in the dark. He had to know for himself. Did his dad really kill his mother. Ashley was a basket case. When she didn't have to attend court and testify, she spent time in her room crying. She and her brother had also grown further apart, the murder case only drove the wedge between them even deeper.

Chapter Fifty

Murder Unresolved

Being afflicted with wanderlust, I traveled as much as I could in my retirement years. I tried working a couple of part-time gigs that didn't pay much money but gave me something to do in my spare time. I had a thirst for and an interest in wine so I signed up and completed the first year to become a sommelier. It didn't seem I had the pallet for such a job and the second year would interfere with my future travel plans so I nixed the idea.

After a couple years of traversing North America on my Harley, and visiting exotic destinations around the world, friends coaxed me into putting my travel tales into a book. I had no intentions of becoming a writer but interest in my work gave me inspiration to write about my career in policing. I wasn't a big reader at the time but a fan of Joseph Wambaugh, a former Los Angeles police detective who became famous for his crime stories.

To my surprise, Wambaugh answered my email and offered me advice on my new hobby. I started a crime series, using my personal notes and own stories to write fiction novels. It was a challenging and learning process that continues today. My books have been well received and my new hobby produces about one book per year. I still find plenty of time to travel.

I was peddling my crime novels at a local book show one day, when Jimmy Gladstone approached my table and said he was a fan of my writing. I hadn't seen him in quite some time and asked how he was doing. While I pictured his sister, Annie, in the back of my mind, Jimmy said how he'd taken over the family business but was working toward retirement himself. His son was helping out and the plan was for him to take over when Jimmy packed it in.

He browsed my selection of titles and I pitched him on my latest work. Then Jimmy said, "You should write about my sister."

I was taken aback and didn't know what to say. A bit embarrassed that I didn't even know the outcome of the murder case, I was afraid to ask. But I did. "Whatever happened with all that?"

Not knowing what I knew, Jimmy answered, "The fucker got away with it...we know her husband killed her, but they let him go."

I was dumfounded and remained silent while he unloaded. I couldn't believe that many years had passed without an arrest in the case and that the suspected killer walked away a free man. The pain was still visible in Jimmy's eyes and taught face. I couldn't imagine how he'd dealt with it all those years.

He went on to say the tragedy basically killed his mother and his father wasn't too far behind her. His words told me life went on but the slouch in his demeanor said Annie's loss would never be forgotten. Another reader stopped at my table and picked up a book. Jimmy took a breath and read the back cover of my latest title.

He bought the book and moved on down the row of authors without receiving an answer from me. I didn't give his suggestion much thought at the time. Jimmy smiled and waved on his way out the door. I watched him move. He looked similar to the man I'd met so many years earlier. But he dragged his feet when he walked, as if something heavy was slowing him down.

Chapter Fifty One

Karma

Dale Daniels was a free man. Rightly so if he wasn't guilty of killing his wife. It also could be said he pulled off the perfect murder and got away with it. We may never know for sure. The media swarmed him and his lawyer when he exited the courthouse. Offering only a brief statement, he said he was happy to get on with his life. He apologized for nothing and didn't bother to reaffirm his innocence.

He relied on Richard Morris to give a song and dance, blaming the Queen's Regional Police investigators for having tunnel vision and focusing only on his client. The veteran lawyer went on to say how the Crown didn't prove their case, practically saying they never should have charged Daniels in the first place. Morris may have worked the case pro-Bono but he gained plenty of media attention during the whole ordeal. Free advertising.

The man who might have gotten away with murder returned to his home up north, where he tried his hand at yet another business. The small town where he was previously unknown became even smaller. Those he'd called friends shied away from him and others stared or whispered about the suspected killer who now roamed their quiet streets.

The relationship with Louise Nantais was long over—she never bothered to wait for Daniels after he was incarcerated. Another failed relationship followed his release, when a jailhouse groupie realized he really wasn't a popular celebrity. Dale's mother passed while he was in custody so he really had no family left.

He offered his children a chance to come home but Christopher had enough and refused the offer. Ashley was torn, still uncertain of whom to believe and that her own father could have killed her mother. She moved back in for a while but kept her distance and remained in a depressed state. She and Christopher rarely spoke and she only talked to the Gladstone's when they reached out.

Daniels had financial problems too. Although he'd raided their joint bank accounts and took or sold whatever else he absconded with when Annie passed, the man was broke. Debts from failed businesses only compounded his situation. Stress, along with mental and physical ailments saw his health decline throughout the whole ordeal. Daniels looked twenty-five years older when he commented on his release on the courthouse steps.

Dale moved again, in search of a place where he could once again start a new life. But no matter where he settled, it seemed people were either staring or talking about him. He constantly looked over his shoulder, forever wondering if the cops were still watching and trying to find another way to take him down. He never spoke again to his one-time family, the Gladstones.

Then one day, he got a call from a buddy he used to jam with. The guy's band was in need of a guitar player for a month-long gig in Toronto. Dale didn't think he was good enough to play in a band on stage, but it was his chance to be the rock star he'd always dreamed of. Giddy as child seeing the ice cream truck coming down the road, Daniels accepted his friend's offer and made plans to meet him in Hog town.

Arriving a day before the gig, Dale worried there wouldn't be enough time to practice with the band. His buddy told him he'd recognize their playlist and he'd only be playing rhythm guitar so he could pick up on the chords while they played. With all that had gone on in his life, Dale hoped his lack of playing time wouldn't show up in his performance.

The day of the gig Daniels purposely slept in, knowing he'd be up late that night with the band. Feeling well-rested, he was surprised he hadn't dreamt about Annie. It was a re-curring dream he couldn't shake, sometimes seeming so real he'd wake up expecting her to be standing in the room. Ac-tually, it was more of a nightmare. She always looked like a zombie from the walking dead, covered in blood with a gap-ing head wound.

Considering the high cost and lack of parking downtown, Dale found a cheap motel close enough to the bar he could walk there. He'd spotted an all-day breakfast joint nearby on King Street, when he checked into the motel. With time to spare before practice with the band, Daniels headed to the restaurant on foot.

Strange, he thought, there was a woman across the street that looked just like Annie. *For Christ's sake, is she haunting me.* The lookalike disappeared into flow of pedestrians on the sidewalk. Dale had to cross over to that side and checked the traffic lights when he got to the corner. There was no walk signal but he saw other pedestrians crossing the intersection diagonally. He started into the roadway.

Halfway across, Dale thought he heard Annie's voice calling to him. He turned around and saw the same woman on the sidewalk where he had just come from. Then she was gone again. *Shit, she really is haunting me.* When Dale turned back around, he saw a bus coming right at him—he'd walked into its path and it wasn't slowing down.

For reasons unknown, Dale froze and wasn't sure which way to go. If he continued in the same direction the bus driver would surely see him and slow enough that he could make it to the curb. Having decided, Dale tried to move but his legs didn't work. It was if his shoes were glued to the pavement. The bus driver blew the horn.

Why can't I move? He heard Annie's voice again. She was laughing. There was no time to look for her, he had to get off the road. Dale grabbed a leg and tried to force it into motion. Time slowed. The pavement blurred and he couldn't see his feet. It was like they'd sunken into the asphalt. *What's happening to me?* He glanced at the bus. It was close enough to see the driver's eyes were the size of avocados.

Dale Daniels panicked and checked his legs again. They were gone. *Fuck!* A feeling of dread swept over him. He still couldn't move. Like he was in quicksand.

The End

About the Author

Edmond Gagnon grew up in Windsor, Ontario, and joined the Windsor Police Department in 1977. Starting as a cadet, Ed was later promoted to constable in the uniform division, where he walked a beat and then worked in patrol cars for the next thirteen years.

He was transferred to plain clothes, working in narcotics, morality, property crime fraud and arson. Promoted to sergeant and then detective, Ed investigated everything from theft and burglary to arson and murder. He retired after accumulating thirty-one years and four months of service.

Within weeks of retirement, Ed took to traveling the world, visiting exotic places in Southeast Asia and South America. He took motorcycle trips all over Canada and the United States. Recipients of Ed's travel e-mail suggested he put his collection of stories into a book. Thus, Edmond Gagnon's first book, *A Casual Traveler,* was born.

Following the success of that book, Ed decided to share some of his police stories. Inspired by events personally experienced and people he met during his career, Edmond Gagnon started the Norm Strom Crime Series with his next book, *Rat.*

Having many more stories to tell, Ed continued the series with *Bloody Friday, Torch,* and *Finding Hope.* After introducing Detroit homicide investigator Abigail Brown in *Border City Chronicles,* he started the Abigail Brown Crime Series and wrote *Moon Mask* - the sequel to *Finding Hope*, and then, *The Millionaire Murders.*

Edmond Gagnon also wrote a paranormal thriller called, *Four.* He continues to write novels in both crime series' and travels frequently with his wife, Cathryn.

All of Edmond Gagnon's books, and more, can be seen on his website: www.edmondgagnon.com

www.ingramcontent.com/pod-product-compliance
Lightning Source LLC
Chambersburg PA
CBHW030250130626
46549CB00002B/473